WOMEN'S PARTICIPATION IN NATURAL RESOURCE MANAGEMENT

WOMEN'S PARTICIPATION IN NATURAL RESOURCE MANAGEMENT

Himanshu Bourai

ABHIJEET PUBLICATIONS
DELHI 110 094

ABHIJEET PUBLICATIONS
2/46 Tukhmeerpur Extension
Delhi-110 094
Phone: 011-22960492, 65698474
E-mail: abhijeetpublication@gmail.com

WOMEN'S PARTICIPATION IN NATURAL RESOURCE MANAGEMENT

First Published 2008

ISBN 978-81-88683-31-8

PRINTED IN INDIA

Published by J.K. Singh for Abhijeet Publications, Delhi-110 094, Lasertypeset by Gaurav Graphices, New Delhi and Printed at Himanshu Printers, Delhi.

Dedicated to

My Niece

GAURI BOURAI

(2 August 1999-31 December 2006)

Aknowledgements

Author is greatly indebted to Dr. J.S. Samra, D.D.G., ICAR who is the real crusader for women participation in watershed management and other development programmes. He is the person who is conceptualizing gender issue in WSM. Dr. V.N. Sharda present Director, CSWCRTI, Dehradun provided valuable guidance and support within the Institute for which I shall always remain thankful to him. I am grateful to Dr. B.L. Dhyani, Sr. Scientist in Economics whose devotion and dedication for common man is well known in Garhwal Himalaya, for his valuable suggestions to me time to time.

I am also thankful to Sr. Scientist, Sr. S.S. Shrimali to providing me all computer facilities in computer lab. I would like to express my sincere thanks to Dr. J.P. Singh, Officer-Incharge, Library and Mrs. Seema Khanna, Library Asstt. to their kind co-operation in library. My thanks to Versha Naithani, Senior Research Fellow (GIS) for her remarkable co-operation in GIS work. I am also thankful to Ambe Enterprises for typing work.

I am grateful to Dr. R.K. Aggarwal, Dr. S.P. Mittal and Dr. Swarnlata Arya in Chandigarh Centre, who helped me a lot during my stayat Chandigarh for field work. Dr. Arya's generous attitude towards me was remarkable. I am thankful to Mrs. Nirmala Sarhadi, T-7 Home Science, Mr. A.N. Gupta, T-2 and Mr. Sunil Kumar, LDC at Chandigarh. I am also thankful to Ms. Jyotsna Sithling (IFS), Dy. Project Director, Doon Valley Watershed Project and Mr. M.S. Yadav, Mr. K.P. Singh, Km. Poonam and Surekha. In Bhuvneshwari Mahila Ashram, NGO, Dr. D.S. Rawat (Geo hydrologist) and his staff co-operate me in field work, for that I am thankful to this NGO. I am also thankful to Madhu Mishra for her contribution in data analysis. My special thanks to Sh. Samudri Singh, (DFO Ropar) for providing accommondation facilities during my stay at Ropar.

Special acknowledgements to ICAR New Delhi & CSWCRTI Dehradun.

Himanshu Bourai

Contents

1

Background

Mahatma Gandhi was a great crusader for the emancipation of women in India. He wrote, "I am uncompromising in the matter of women's rights. In my opinion she should labour under no legal difficulty not suffered by men. They (women) can no longer be treated as dolls or slaves without the social body remaining in a condition of social pararalysis. This is why I take every occasion to protest in no uncertain terms that so long as women in India remain ever so little suppressed or do not have the same rights (as men) India will not make real progress". Mahatma was a person of high ethical values, but also a great mobiliser of masses for the goal of winning freedom. As a leader of masses we clearly saw that these popular movements would not succeed unless women got involved of their free will in large numbers, cutting across classes and castes, breaking as under the age old shackles of customs and religious practices which confined them to their homes and families. Women could take decision to join the mass movement only if they had autonomy which meant smashing the fetters that put them in a position of subordination and made them play an inferior role. Mahatmaji asserted "so long as women in India do not take equal part with men in the affairs of the world and in religious and political matters we shall not see India's star rising".

Women in India: An Overview

The All India Congress Committee constituted study groups on women issues in the twenties and early thirties. In the Karachi session of the Indian National Congress in 1931 a resolution was adopted of fundamental rights which incorporated the concept of equality of sexes. The national planning committee constituted by Subhash Chandra Bose under the Chairmanship of Jawaharlal Nehru prepared a report on the women question highlighting many of the modern day concepts of equality of sexes and gender justice.

The National Planning Committee, under the chairmanship of Pandit Jawaharlal Nehru, had formed a number of sub-committee to deal with all aspects of national life. A sub-committee was also appointed to deal with the place of women in the planned economy of India, including consideration of her social, economic and legal status, her right to hold any property, carry on any trade, profession or occupation and remove all obstacles or handicaps in obstacles or handicaps in the way of realizing an equal status and opportunity for women. The sub-committee has touched almost every aspect of women's life and role in the national development.

The liberal ideas of Pandit Jawaharlal Nehru and his far-sighted vision of his country emerging as a strong developed nation is very much evident in the 'status' and 'role' he accords to the 'women' in the planned economy. The following lines bear ample evidence of the lofty objectives of the sub-committee:

"We have touched in this report upon subjects which are delicate and controversial, as the very nature of this work has demanded a scrutiny of all problems connected with the social order. An essential characteristic of our time is the rational application of scientific thought and experience to all vital problems; and it is in this spirit, desirous of finding practical solutions, that we have tried, to approach each subject."

"Circumstances have altered so radically in recent years that the old frame no longer fits the new picture, and hence it has become necessary to make some changes. This does not imply condemnation. It merely seeks to make the system more fitted for the task before it, by an effort of conscious planning. It is not our desire to belittle in any way those traditions, which have in the past, contributed to the happiness and progress of the individuals, and have been the means, of raising the dignity and beauty of Indian womanhood and conserving the spiritual attributes of the Indian Nation. We do not wish to turn women into a cheap imitation of man or to render her useless for the great tasks of motherhood and nation building. But in demanding equal status and equal opportunity we desire to achieve for women the possibility of development under favourable circumstances of education and opportunity and while so doing, urge upon the state its responsibility towards women in this respect.

This main purpose in quoting so extensively the objectives of the sub-committee is to impress the point that the importance in the planned economy of the country, had been, recognised and given considerable though by the early patriots and planners. Their recommendations have been indeed very comprehensive and touch almost every sphere of women's social and economic activities. After nearly five decades of planning, the recommendations of the sub-committeee any significant impact on the development of the women. The economic imbalances under which they laboured have not altered much and the social changes that were expected to precede the economic development have not come off. In some areas, much to the dismay social imbalances have even widened?

The increasing inequalities between the rich and the poor and the yawning gap between development in rural and urban areas has been causing great concern in recent times. This is very much evident from the growing unrest among the agricultural labourers and 'outbursts' rural areas.

So in the process of identifying some of the causes for the failures of our plans and programmes, it has been increasingly realized that the rural women in particular who constitute quite a sizeable section of who have been contributing actively at every stages of agricultural production have been mostly overlooked in the sharing of the fruits of their labour. Besides, the changes in the process of agricultural development has been affecting them even adversely in some cases, depriving them of employment opportunities and means of livelihood. The target group approach certain particular sections of the society especially women and integrate them in the development process has been engaging much attention of our planners and policy makers in recent years, in order to bring development.

The Preamble to the Constitution assures justice, social, economic and political equality of status and opportunity and dignity of the individual. The fundamental rights guarantee women's equality under law.

The Balwantray Mehta Committee (1957) which examined the working of community projects and national extension service had suggested that: (1) the care of the cow, the kitchen garden and poultry should receive primary of attention of women workers in the villagers; (2) training in elementary use of thread and needle should be given so that women can sew clothes for the family; (3) in village surrounding large towns and cities, cookery classes should be started.

The community development programme accorded in important role to the organisation of women, who constitute nearly so percent of our population, so that their enthusiastic participation in rural development was effectively ensured. These organisations of women, known as Mahila Mandals, came to be established in a phased in different status. The broad objectives of these mandals, as outlined in several documents, were: (1) To help women to participate in development programmes; (2) To act an agency for planning, developing and executing programmes for women and children; (3) To provide opportunities for discussing their needs and problems and share responsibilities with other according to their interests and abilities; (4) To help them understand their roles and responsibilities; (5) To faster group effort in the implementation of activities; (6) To develop different kind of activities for the common good; and (7) to develop leadership among women.

At the conference held at New Delhi (Development

Commissioners) in 1963, it was decided that ultimately there should be one Mahila Mandal in each village and that priority should be given to the economic programmes, like horticulture, pisciculture, piggery, poultry, bee-keeping, food processing and preservation, sericulture, kitchen gardening and tailoring.

The working group (1978) constituted for reviewing the objectives and functioning of Mahila Mandals has recommended a new programme, in keeping with the new development observed, "is to draw rural women into the mainstream of development and to enable them to function as instruments of social change by providing them with programme which they will have a stake or a sustained interest such as improving their income or productivity and employability or employment. Calling for a flexible approach in regard to the type of women is organizations in order to meet the needs of different sections of society, it recommended: (1) The establishment of one Mahila Mandal for every unit of 500 people; (2) making a block grant of Rs. 1,500 to each Mahila Mandal for administrative and economic development purposes, respectively, (The latter has to be sanctioned depending on the quality and size of the project planned by the mandal); (3) The training of village level organizer to promote and help the mandal; (4) The posting of five field level workers per block and one officer each at the block, district and state levels; (5) giving representation to mandals in the panchayats; and (6) the formation of federation of Mahila Mandals at the block and district levels.

The Ashok Mehta Committee on Panchayati Raj Institutions (1978) recommended that the programme for women "should recognize and strength their constructive, decision making and managerial roles so as the enable them to have full access to development resources and services". Emphasizing on the importance of the motivational and promotional role of panchayati raj bodies in the women's programme, the committee recommended for a committee with all women members of the proposed mandal panchayat represented in it so that decisions on priorities and choice in welfare and development programmes mental for them were made by themselves.

The working group (1978) constituted for reviewing the objectives and functioning of the village-level organizations took note of the slow progress of Mahila Mandals and listed following reasons therefore: (1) lack of clarity in objectives and of appreciation of women's multiple roles within and outside the home; (2) difficulties in identifying target groups and inability to reach the poorest sections; (3) neglect of economic activity or training in productive skills; (4) multiplicity of programmes and agencies with sectional approaches and limited objectives resulting in uncoordinated diffusion of resources, inadequate coverage and absence of an integrated policy or approach; (5) lack of properly qualified field staff and inadequate provision of supervisory staff; (6) failure to mobilize effective and sustained support of men to rural women's programmes and absence of appropriate linkages with local institutions like Panchayats, Zilla Parishads; and (7) rigidity in design and structure of the programmes leaving little room for local initiative or identification of needs.

The foregoing review of the available literature clearly shows that the performance of the Mahila Mandal has been far from being satisfactory. These organizations have yet to play their role as instruments of change in the overall strategy of rural development. It is also noticed that the Mahila Mandals have yet to be recognised as an integral part of the total rural development policy. The main reasons for their poor performance have been identified as inadequacy of staff, vagueness in objectives, lack of financial support, lack of participation of all section of women, and above all, lack of an appropriate policy approach.

The emphasis has been mostly on social and cultural activities and very little economic orientation has so far been given.

But in the seventies report of the committee on the status of women in India clearly pointed out that the Indian State had failed in its constitutional obligation of not discriminating on ground of gender. There was no acknowledgement of the fact that millions of women in India earn their livelihood in developing sectors like agriculture, industry, furnishes, livestock etc. Impact the report showed however, the period of planned development employment of women came down sharply in some organised industries. Sadly the planners increasingly viewed that women were not in need of independent avocations to the point, where women's decreasing work participation and share of employment, increasing poverty and economic and social in security in sectors where hey had dominated earlier were not even viewed as problems to be dealt with. This process of marginalisation of a large majority of women in the economy and their consequent neglect and devaluation by society and the state were a clear indication of the overriding game a wide mandate to the notwithstanding the pro-women pressures in the constitution gave a wide mandate to the govt. "to remove all disabilities that India women continue to suffer from."

UN-Decade for Women

In 1972, the year of the Stockholm conference on the human environment, the General Assembly of the United Nations proclaimed 1975 International Women's Year. That year, UN decided, would be devoted to integration action to promote between men and women, to ensure the full integration of women in the total development effort and to increase women's contributions to the strengthening of World peace.

A World Conference on the International Women's Year was held Mexico in 1975. Adopted a world action plan to implement the objectives of the year and proclaimed the period 1976-1985 the UN Decade for Women. Another Conference was held in Copenhagen in 1980, midway through the decade and on action plan for the next five years was agreed upon. In July 1985, the World Conference to review and appraise the achievements of the UN Decade for Women: equality, development and peace were held in Nairobi.

Representative of 157 countries and 263 non-governmental organizations attended the Nairobi Conference, which had two principal goals, to review achievement of the decade and discuss the obstacles to further success and to develop future strategies. Forward looking strategies for the advancement of women formed the final document of the Conference.

Environmental Concern

Representatives of several UN agencies, including

UNEP, UNDP and WHO focused on the relationship between women and the environment and the problems environmental degradation posses for them. In the Nairobi declaration deep concern was expressed over the profound economic and social crisis that women and children were experiencing, especially in Africa, as a result of severe drought, famine, external debt and the effects of the international economic situation. A key resolution generated at the conference and later adopted by the UN General Assembly, urged; international agencies to provide more information on women's role in conservation; that governments take environment factors into consideration in their development projects: Those social as well as economic criteria are applied to development; and that sustainable development is promoted.

The main outcome of Nairobi Conference, however, was the document forward looking strategies for the advancement of women, which was accepted by all 157 countries and later adopted, without a vote, by the 40th session of the UN General Assembly in resolution 40108 on 13th December, 1985. It dealt with a range of issues; equality, development (including agriculture, science and technology, housing, energy, environment, education employment, health industry, trade and commercial services, communication and social services), peace, international and regional co-operation and social areas of concern (such as women in drought area, the urban poor elderly and young women, women deprived women). But what signaled a change was the fact that, for the first time in the history of the woman decade, the issue of the environment as it related to women was taken up. The relevant sections, adopted by consensus, are:

Deprivation of traditional means of livelihood is most often a result of environmental degradation resulting from such natural and man made disasters as droughts, floods, hurricans, erosion, desertification and inappropriate land use. Such conditions have already pushed great numbers of poor women into marginal environments where critically low levels of water supplies, shortages of fuel, over utilization of growing and arable lands and population density have deprived them of their livelihood. Most seriously affected are the women in drought affiliated arid and semi-arid areas and in urban slums and squatter settlements. These women need options for alternative means of livelihood. Women must have the same opportunity, as men to participate in the wage-earning labour force in such programmes as irrigation and tree planting and in other programmes needed to upgrade international economic co-operation in the exploration of water resources and the control of desertification and other environmental disasters. (Paragraph 224)

Efforts to improve sanitary conditions, including drinking water supplied organizations of environmental issues and the capacity of women and men to manage their environment and sustain productive resources should be enhanced.

All sources of information and dissemination should be mobilized to increase the self-help potential of women in conserving and improving their environment. National and international emphasis on ecosystem management and the control of environmental degradation should be strengthened and women should be recognised as active and equal participants in this process (paragraph 226)

The environmental impact of policies, programmes and projects on women's health and activities, including their sources of employment and income, should be assessed and the negative effects eliminated (paragraph 227)

Implementation of the objectives of the decade on equality, development and peace and of the resolutions in forward-looking strategies will be monitored over the year 1986 to 2000 both national and international levels.

Central in this review and appraisal will be the UN Commission on the Status of Women, established by the UN Economic and Social Council in June 1946. The Commissioner's mandate is to prepare recommendations and reports on the promotion of women's rights in political, social and educational fields. In 1967, the commission adopted the declaration on the elimination of discrimination against women, which was approved by the general Assembly in 1979 and came into force in 1981.

Other specialized United Nations agencies which focus particularly on the role and position of the women are the UN Development Fund for Women (UNIFEM), the International Research and Training Institute for the Advancement of Women at the Centre for social development advance humanitarian affairs.

But, like all international movements for change, it will take time for the recommendations of the women's decade to become a reality and for the benefits to be realised at the local level. Meanwhile, other international organizations are beginning to recognize the crucial part that women play in environment management.

Women and IUCN (International Union for Conservation of Nature and Natural Resources)

At IUCN's 16th General Assembly in Madrid in 1984, a recommendation was put forward to guarantee better representation of women and women's issues in its work. As the then president, Mohammed Kassas, said:

> "We are yet to achieve true participation of women in the work of the union. Few women been invited to lead discussions at this General Assembly and I would like us to look into prospectus and means for bringing women all over the World into the movement. Let us all take this mission to heart".

The representation of professional women in development organisation is important. But more crucial is that the Donor and policy-making organisations have a proper focus on the role and position of the women. Some IUCN documents such as the Union's Bulletin do this. The IUCN Sahel reports, under the heading "Promoting New styles of development at the national and international level".

New perceptions of the role of women are crucial for a re-evaluation of the contribution of major groups who have been historically disadvantaged. These include especially women and children who constitute the majority of the rural population as a result of socio-economic forces, particularly rural-urban migration.

Care should be taken to avoid gender segregation that will be counter producing women's actual economic and social activities, including farming of food crops, rather than pre-conceived India about their feminine role, should be targeted for particular assistance (IUCN, 1986).

1. A crucial ingredient for success is that projects should be locally designed and locally managed.
2. Local knowledge, low cost local tools and materials controlled by villagers.
3. Women's groups have been especially effective in mobilising support for conserving activities.
4. Women must have legal and secure rights to cultivate land.
5. "The approach," says Harrison, is basic and unglamorous.
6. Women must be a target group for training. Studies by the International labour organisation suggest that working with women separately is often necessary to ensure they are reached by training programmes. Further, local training works best where it is augmented by government extension programmes (where more women must be recruited), and by communications on radio and in the press. It helps where there are networks of school and youth clubs promoting similar messages, as is the practice in the wildlife clubs of Kenya and Zambia. Training workshops, distribution of training materials, farm local networks for "primary environment care'". Spreading conservation messages suing modern audio-visual methods as well as the traditional media of stories and songs, dance and drama.

Women are still not well represented among senior decision-makers in development institutions. Brudtland says, "Women are used to think in the long term".

Yet at the top as at the grassroots, they are not listened to. The need is for national or regional focal points. With a funded secretariat, to form alliances of environmental and welfare NGOs, research and educational institutions and women's groups which can argue against misguided projects and press for sustainable development action. Where their dignity and confidence have been restored, women have shown they can act decisively; they do have some thing to say". (Irene Dankelmen and Joan Davidson)

The Concept of Development

The concept of development involves economic and social factors as moral and cultural values on which depend the full development of the human personality and the dignity of man in society. We agree with Malcolm Adiseshiah when he succinctly remarks:

> "Development is a function of series of variables and not just of the economic variables of industrialization, urbanization, international trade and national income level; but also of the enlightenment variables of schooling, literacy and media exposure, the power variables of participation, party membership and voting; the personality variables of motivation, need achievement and sympathy; the diversity of cultural variables of local temporal aspects of social cultural behaviour and the ecological variables of population, organisation, environment and technology together with principles of interdependence, and differentiation development must thus be conceived in a holistic, organic, dynamic, valuational manner.

Its planning requires human centered approach".[1]

We consider modernization as an integral part of the development process but development is not just modernization. Modernization, like development, is a unique and thorough going transformation of society involving changes in all spheres at social and individual levels. In the economic sphere, it is related to industrialization by the application of science and technology; in the political sphere it means increased participation of citizens in the development process: and in the socio-psychological realm, it modifies attitudes, beliefs, values and behaviour and accelerates urbanization, literacy and mobility. Development embodies all these process but it is something wider and much more than modernization. It is also a dialectical rather than unilinear. Process because it inevitably releases opposing forces and it involves ethical and normative considerations. It involves a complex of mutually related economic, social and political, administrative changes the state society, administration and people. The national and international community, the north and the south have to play an increasing role in resolving the challenges of the societal trams formation for national building and socio-economic programmes. It is in this context people's participation in the development process assumes fundamental importance.

In the Indian context, development means the banishment of inequality, poverty and unemployment through peaceful democratic means and full participation of the people in the decisional network.

The Concept of People Participation

In developing democracies like India, the realization of true, democracy and attainment of national integration and socio-economic development administration hinges upon the active participation and involvement of people in the affairs of the state. Citizen participation is the means of attainment of national goals and decentralization—political and administrative is the means of promoting people's participation and cooperation in democratic development. There exists a triangular relationship between decentralization, democracy and development.[2] Institution of local self-government signifying political decentralization are essential for development for they alone make popular participation in decision making effective and informed. Further, achievement of social change and economic growth requires a spreading of efforts so that local communities and individuals can participate and bring under ideal conditions energy, enthusiasm and local initiative to the working out of local developmental activities. On the other hand, it is only when people have control over decisions and their execution that administration had become responsible and responsive to people's needs and aspirations. As the UN document specified:

> An important reason for decentralization is to develop more effective popular participation in local government that is carried out locally. Such participation not only enhances the dignity of the individual and the sense of community at all levels, but also adds vitality to governmental programmes and provides a means for local control over them. It makes the programmes

more responsible and better adopted to local needs. Moreover, through participation, members of the community may be induced to do more on their own initiative and make a fuller contribution to government programmes.[3] Participation is an action–oriented term. It calls for drive. Will and skill on the part of the participant citizen or group to be actively involved in the development activities. At the same time, participation differs from mobilisation in that the latter involves an element of force or compulsion and gives no share to the citizen of the public to influence decision i.e., in determining plan priorities or allocation of resources or setting up of goals. In other words, the mobilization model like that of Karl Deutsch and others is based on the assumption that the people are incapable of articulating their needs and aspirations and that the task has to be left to the elite group in bureaucracy and politics. Vital decisions concerning development goals, plan objectives and priorities, resources allocation and strategies "is not an unitary event but the product of a complex social process generally extending over a consideration period of time—decision making includes that determine the actions of decisions, processes for discovering and designing possible courses of actions and process for evolving alternatives and choosing among them for Peter Drucker the decisional process involves five steps, viz., (a) defining the problem, (b) analysing it, (c) developing alternative, solutions, (d) finding the best solution and (e) finally making decisions effectives by converting it into action.

The participation of citizens i.e. the target group in each of these phases is essential for the attainment of plan objectives and goals on which depends the development of the groups concerned. The participation of the target population in the decisional process is vital because as Haldipur observes, all decisions affect human beings as they are taken to enhance the quality of human life. Somebody is going to work and some persons are going to be affected by it and therefore, it has to be participative, and in this the citizen cannot be left out as bystander.

Feminist sociologist Dorothy Smith has suggested that good sociology must rely on everyday live and lived experience as sources for the communication of our problematic and sociological knowledge. She believes that feminist where must be an insider's sociology where knowledge comes from the people who are living the life, and which includes both the subject of research and the researcher (I took these words to heart).

In Himachal Pradesh, however, development, or capitalist transformation, had not in any way improved living conditions for the people in the area and had, instead considerably depleted the natural resources of the area. Not surprisingly, this had a deleterious effect on the lives of the people who depended on natural resources for their livelihoods. Forestry development, in particular, had deeply affected the lives of women from the poor, peasant classes because of their close relationship to the forest and their dependence on the environment to meet daily household needs. It is very clear that in India as in any other parts of the developing world environmental issues and women's issues are inseparable.

Theoretically speaking or as a point of departure for social inquiry, Sen, Gita and Grown (1987) have suggested reasons for starting from the ventage point or standpoint of women, poor women in particular. First women make up the majority of the poor, socially disadvantaged in most societies. Therefore any development that produces an improvement in the standard of living, alleviates poverty, provides access to employment and reduces inequalities should start with women, since this will lead to an improvement in the general standard of everyone is necessary for the survival and reproduction of the family in all societies. In India, in particular, as in many other parts of the third world poor women are responsible for domestic food production and processing, fuel and water collection, health care and child-rearing. As such, their lives and specific viewpoints with respect to the implementation of development programme are vital. It is their daily lives which stand to be affected most deeply by the success or failure of these programmes.

The recent literature on women's participation in development or income generating programmes in India is inclined to be more quantitative than qualitative and based on economic transformation. It neglects women's viewpoint and focuses on issues at the macro level. A study in Solan district titled "Men, Women and the Forest: Two Villages of Himachal Pradesh" by Sarin and Guhathakurta (1992) is a good example of this. Other examples include Dhiman (1989), Tiwari (1993), Sarin (1989) and Vaidya and Sikka (1991). A general analysis of social forestry from the framework of political economic is valuable but it should also include a gendered analysis as well as qualitative data, thereby providing an integrated and inclusive theory.

A gendered analysis is in fact, imperative as men and women are affected in different ways by development prospects. For example, as women are responsible for subsistence needs such as fodder and fuel wood collection, their relationship to social forestry prospects in necessarily different from men's. (Brenda Cranney)

When looking at the impact of development forest such as social forestry, it is also important to analyse changes in the quality of life of poor people and especially in terms of the quality of life of women. Quantitative research and analysis alone do not accomplish this effectively. In fact, a quantitative approach shows that income-generating projects are successful when, in reality, the quality of life of poor women has diminished. The food and agriculture organisation forestry paper 75, 'monitoring and evaluation of social forestry in India: An operational Guide' (1886), provides a useful evaluation of the economic success of social forestry but is lacking any qualitative assessment of the success of forestry project. The voices of the women who were affected by such projects were never heard. Instead, what was stressed was the number and suitability of seedlings for plantations. Suitability was not based on what kind of species the women wanted for fuel and fodder but on market requirements (cash crops). Bina Agrawal's (1989) Article "Under the cooking pot; the political economy of the domestic fuel crisis in Rural South Asia and Schrijvers 1988 article Blueprint for undernourishment: The Mahawali River development scheme in Sri Lanka' effectively demonstrate that economic success does not necessarily mean betterment for women. It is important to connect the seemingly secondary issues of women's day-to-day lives to the broader picture of capitalist transformation. In doing so the relationship between economy, political and lived experience become tangible. This necessarily involves looking at women's lives as a direct result of their relationship to their local environment. Furthermore, by focusing on the micro level of everyday life, it is possible to gain another perspective on the macro level, which many studies neglect.

The food/fuel/water crisis currently affecting the hill region of India, and specifically region like Uttarakhand and Shiwalik has it origins in the early developments of the colonial period and is perpetuated by development politics today. The exploitation of forests has taken two forms, commercial felling and monoculture plantation. Commercial felling has in fact resulted in India losing 1-3 million hectares of forests each year in the period from 1975 to 1982 (Agrawal, and Narain 1986:80). As a result of deforestation and monoculture 'plantation' agriculture these has been an extreme loss of ground water, along with flooding, landslides, and the destruction of biomass. Biomass-including food, fodder, fertilizer (forest litter, manure), building materials and medicinal herbs-plays a crucial role in meeting daily survival needs of most of the rural population (*Ibid:* 172). The failure of social forestry projects in many parts of India is, thus, for the most part, a result of overemphasis on commercialization: The unwillingness of these projects to address structural changes, i.e. property relations, such as land holdings; and the use of a top-down approach for project identification, planning and implementation (Sen, Gita and Grown). In hills there is an added dimension to the failure of social forestry—the total disregard of a 'mountain' perspective. Projects are implemented as if there were no differences between conditions in the mountains and on the plains. Not only have the projects failed in making conditions better for people who live in the areas affected by the programmes, but the natural environment has deteriorated as well.

Women's health is also affected by the environmental degradation. Increased work load taken its toll on their physical stamina and well-being as they must work harder to achieve a minimum subsistence level. Many women suffer from back problems due to the heavy loads that they carry from an early age. Food is not as plentiful an, as research shows, women's food a shortage (Agarwal, B. 1989; Batliwala 1985; Chen, L. 1981; Schrijvers 1988). The lack of fuel wood is also directly linked to malnutrition as more nutritious foods are substituted with those that require less cooking.

Formulation of resources-based development policies should be based on environmental protection, bio-resources conservation and sustainable use, local communities participation and benefits, it should consider their knowledge and culture and be maintained over a period of time in the face of multiple claims. Wherever the water harvesting structure failed miserably, the local people's wisdom and experiences were not taken into consideration. In most of the cases, structures were designed and implemented ignoring indigenous knowledge and skills one of the important regions for the failures of dams and the faulty designs and wrong selection of the sites were also taken in notice. (Brenda Cranney)

Natural Resources Degradation

The simultaneous explosion in population and land degradation are the two basic agrarian problems of India, which have defied solution thus far. Most of India lies in the semi-arid topics and 74 percent of the arable land is rainfed which contribute 45 percent to the national food production (Anonymous, 1976). The demands on the farm and forestland are increasing and so are the threats of land degradation of the total 329 million hectare (mha) land area of the country 80 mha are threatened by water erosion. 20 mha by wind erosion and desertification. 7m ha by excessive salt, 6 mha by water logging and 4 mha by ravines (Anonymous, 1976, Das, 1983 and Tejwani, 1979). As a result of destruction of the forests and natural vegetation, 5334 million tones (16.4 destruction of the forests and natural vegetation, 5334 million tons (16.4 t/ha) of rich soil is being washed to the sea annually which contains 5.4 million tonnes of plant nutrients (Dhruva Narayana and Babu, 1983). Forty million hectares have turned as waste lands. Soil, the very basis for plant life and human survival if one denuded and degraded. The pathway of recovery is rather slow and difficult. The deterioration in the soil fertility, productivity and land qualities has become a matter of serious concern. The efficient management of land and water resources should receive top priority to improve the prospects of increasing and sustaining productivity in the seasonally dry area of India (Swaminathan, 1980). The management approaches shall, however very according to rainfall, soil type, crops grown, and socio economic setting of each agro-ecological region (Tejwani and Gupta, 1975).

The Concept of Watershed Management

After the 73th constitutional amendment watershed development has been included in the schedule of subjects to be handled by Panchayats. This provides opportunity for combining development of grassroots democracy and natural resources in symbiotic manner a watershed is a naturally defined geographical area that drains to a common point. The concept sustainable land management on watershed basis is quite ancient in India. Tank irrigation systems, particularly of south India, construction of Guhls (Water conveyance channels on contours) of Himalayas. Van Panchayats and a great variety of community based non-statutory institutions are few examples of out traditional strength (J.S. Samra).

Excess rainwater after absorption by soil flows as runoff in small gullies, rivulets, streams and join to form a river course. The river basins at macro level and watershed level represent the natural drainage system.

To a commoner watershed is a drainage basis of a stream. Technically watershed is a hydrological entity. It is an area expansion of land from which the runoff flows through a natural drain as gullies or streams or rivers. Therefore, area of land falling on a watershed is hydrologically inter-related in that, it has its own natural drainage system. More than 70 percent of the flowing water is going waste into the seas. This causes extensive flood damage en route, costing the country thousands of crores of rupees in flood damage alleviation annually. (Parthasarathy 2000)

Land degradation is caused by both water and wind erosions at almost extreme hydrological situations of flood and drought, respectively. Hence, if wind and water erosion is controlled, land degradation is avoided or reduced. Watershed management is an integrated approach of conservation of land, water of biomass for ultimate benefit of mankind on the contrary; if the watershed is not managed through effective conservation measures, the land degradation vis-a-vis watershed development is inter-related as both have various spheres of resources protection and development.

Watershed is understood to be a catchment area feeding identifying drainable system, such as a stream or river, watersheds contain a number of biophysical resources: soil and water, along with vegetation in the form of trees, grasses and crops, and also provide livestock production. The idea of watershed management was adopted by multipurpose Damodar Valley development project (Chaitali Pal.). A major policy change was made in 1954 in establishing a chain of soil and water conservation, research, Demonstration and training centers all over India. About 42 micro-watersheds were developed since 1956 with major thrust on biophysical issues especially hydrology. Research findings of this limited experience became basis of lunching river valley projects for conserving various catchments in 1961-62. Another paradigm shift in favour of participatory and demand driven watershed management was initiated by Central Soil and Water Conservation Research and Training Institute, Dehradun during 1974 (J.S. Samra) . The concept had since been reiterated in all plan documents. A series of integrated development projects for local areas were started in early 1980's first by ICAR and later by Ministry of Rural Development, Ministry of Environment and Forests and Ministry of Planning and Programme

Implementation dealing with rural area development, employment, poverty alleviation and watershed development.

Watershed Management

Total water flow through rivers, quantity used and that lost by draining into sea:

Total water flow through rivers in India 1869km^3/ annum

Quantity of water used at present = 550km^3/annum (roughly 30%).

Quantity of water that goes waste into sea = 1319km^3/annum (roughly 70%)

Major Steps of Watershed Development

1. Site selection.
2. Bench mark resource survey.
3. Development of operational WSM Plan.
4. People's participation.
5. Implementation of Plan.
6. Monitoring.
7. Feed back.

Characteristics of Successful Watershed Management

1. The involvement of all sections of the society, including women.
2. Identification of people's priorities.
3. The use of simple but effective technology;

- interventions to manage runoff water
- through watershed development by:
    - (A) Cheap methods
    - (B) Local materials, and
    - (C) Local labour

Watershed management is a holistic and sustained development programme including;

(A) Water management

(B) Community managed erosion prevention and

(C) Widespread afforestation

Forum of Decision Making:

(A) Major decisions should take the Gram Sabha

(B) Institutionalised democratic system of functioning

Implications:

- Full and active participation of local people
- Overall resource conservation
- In building up land-based resources

Management of:

- Crop productively
- Standard of living
- Improvement in socio-economic and environmental conditions.

Institutional level:

1. Planning of watershed management and village people.
2. Decision making and village people.

3. Management of watershed management and village people.

Field level: People problems, needs and interests.

Impact of the watershed management:

How village people benefited from the watershed management

The status of village people:

Control over the resources

- Access to land, labour and credit
- Membership and participation in formal bodies and political institute.
- Work in hours in a day (workload).
- Fodder, fuel wood, water and women.
- Agriculture tasks and women.
- Other activities and village people.

People participation and watershed management: People participation in watershed management is as vital as the scientific input in the planning and designing of the programme. Importance of people's participation in making the programme self sustainable is now widely accepted by the planners, administrators, academicians and practitioners all over the world (B.L. Dhyani). According to Banki (1981), Participation means "a dynamic process in which all member of a work group contribute, share, or are influenced by the interchange of ideas and activities towards problems solving or decision making".

Singh (1990) used this term to "mean the fact act of partaking (by farmers) in all the stage of soil and water conservation programme right from designing of various structures through monitoring and evaluation of their performance."

Participation: (A) Awareness in the community about project, (its objective, politics and results) through film shows farmers meetings, surveys and visit to research farm. (B) Drafting of plan and workout priorities with full involvement of farmers, indigenous knowledge and needs (C) Implementation of maximum possible work in the watershed by involvement of local people.

Purpose of people participation: Extension of modern land management technologies to the farming community. To obtain their willing support in the programme and make integral part of their farming activities. Development of human resource base of watershed. Local institution building for follow up action.

Women development report, 1999 shows India's Gender Related Development Index (GDI) as 0.525 with the rank of 112. We may feel comfortable compared Pakistan (Rank 116), Bhutan (119) and Bangladesh (123). But compared so Sri Lanka (76) and China (79) we are far below. One can feel happy that over the years GDI in India in inching forward. In 1997 rank was 118; undoubtedly there has been some progress, though nothing very significant.

Most rural women are directly dependent on their immediate environment and their own skills in using in, for the daily necessities of life (Recheluae, 1985:8). Women, particularly those living in the rural areas of Third World countries, play a major role in managing natural resources—soil, water, forest and energy. Their tasks in agriculture and animal husbandry as well as in the household make them the daily mangers of the living environment. They have a profound knowledge of the plants, animals and ecological process around them.

Women also participate in the commercial sectors of society and the raw materials they use in rural enterprises are vulnerable to environment degradation and contamination. As farmers and traders, then women experience environmental as directly undermines the basis of their daily lives.

The principal victims of environmental degradation are the most under privileged people and the majority of these are women (Senghor, 1985). Their problems and those of the environment are very must interrelated. Both are marginalized by existing development policies. And because of the complex cycles of poverty, inappropriate development and environmental degradation, poor people have been forced into ways of living which induce further destruction, (Aidoo 1985). Third world women have no choice but to exploit natural resources in order to survive, even though they may have the knowledge to promote sustainability. Women constitute about half the world's population, account for 75% of the working hours, and contribute upto 30% of the official labour force, yet receive only ten per cent of the income and own less than one percent of the world's property. The situation is rather appalling in the developing countries.

They constitute more than half of labour input especially in hilly, rainfed and arid ecosystem where male outmigration elsewhere is quite common for supplementing family income. On the contrary they are inadequately empowered except in matriarchical system of north-west, higher Himalayas of Himachal Pradesh/Uttaranchal and Kerala. Several mechanisms of their empowerment have been provided in the common guidelines. Women's groups have been relatively more successful in credit and thrift societies, silkworm rearing, dairying, raising of nurseries, poultry etc. Improvement in their membership, active participation and actual empowerment was noted in Agha Khan Rural support programme of Gujarat.

J.S. Kanwar said, "I may be wrong but I feel that we have to go back to the villages, Panchayats and individuals farmer or group of farmers or user. The plans must be responsive to their perception, aspirations and needs."

In India, women constitute 48.5% of the rural population. About 75% of the rural women belong to the families of small and marginal farmers. Two third of them are illiterate and provide most of the farm labour by putting in 14-18 hours of productive manual labour. Farm women are the backbone of the India agriculture. Growing food has been as interminable saga of her life. No field operation is beyond her competence. She is at her best is sowing, transplanting, weeding, manuring, winnowing, threshing, storing, marketing, rearing, livestock and poultry. In many of these operations, farm women in India are the backbone the Indian agriculture. Women constitute 48.5 percent of the rural population. She is competent in sowing, harvesting, winnowing, threshing, storing, marketing, rearing livestock and poultry. Although women have never been involved directly as a 'target group' in watershed management programmes in general and soil and water conservation programme in particular, yet these programmes change the stage of natural resources especially that of soil, water and vegetation. Even such an environmental friendly effort may result in increased pressure on farm women. She is more efficient than a man. These operations are performed by farm women over and above the routine household chores which include in but drudgery of cooking meals on a smoky chulha, washing clothes, cleaning utensils and rearing children unhygienically.

Watershed management is now a widely accepted technology for resource management in totality and coherently with people's participation in a holistic manner. Women participation in WSM is an important component of people participation in WSM.

Meaning of Women Participation in WSM

(A) How many women come forward and take part in the preparation of natural management herewith special reference to WSM.

(B) Are the women coming forward and planning to have a management of WS.

(C) Are they convinced that this is what they would like to do, because it would be of help to them and they see watershed as being beneficial both monetarily and from the environment point of view.

(D) Are they taking decisions on the rights of the watershed, on the issues related to management of the WSM?

(E) Does this experience give them the confidence to work on other developmental activities?

(F) Does it increase their confidence and capabilities in dealing with problem situation?

In this Study Border Area

1. This study is concerned with one aspect of "women's role" in watershed management to search.
2. Whether these projects have adequately recognized the role of women in watershed management.
3. How can this potential be best developed in the interest of sound conservation practices? If there are any successful examples from which we can learn.
4. What are the appropriate approaches to the active participation of women in development projects like watershed management and what are the practical examples of these?
5. What are women's specific problems in gaining or retaining access to land or using tree products?
6. What specific time, financial and other factors constrain women participation?
7. What measure ensures that women benefit from project?
8. What different social structures allow participating as individuals or in group?

Methodology

A. Diagnostic survey was conducted on the basis of sample survey in Sukhomajri WSM, Relmajra WSM and Fakot WSM of Central soil and Water Conservation Research and Training Institute, Chandrabadni and Danda WSM of

Bhuvneshwari Mahila Ashram (NGO), Chandrabhaga WSM of State Govt. of Uttar Pradesh now is in Uttaranchal.

B. In these watersheds families were selected for survey on the basis of age group of women and land holding capacities.

C. Total women interviewed on the basis of questioner were 297 between the age group of 20 to 75 and holding the land between < one bigha to 20 bigha and land less also.

D. Focus was on how they are participating in watershed management activities directly or indirectly and how the participation of women can be increased from their point of view.

There are very few standardized methods of understanding and analysing research and extension system. For convenience, Falconer's paradigm is being used, more as a reference point then as a means of arrive at a final conclusion. According to him, "while there are many approaches and numerous methods of research and extension, they be broadly categorised at top down (dictated from outside) versus 'bottom up'/dialogue (planned and managed with local participation and outside advice and guidance) approaches" (Falconer, 1987). They are defined below:

The 'Top Down' Approach

This allows only one way information delivery from research and extension service to rural resource users, where appropriate research topics are often determined by bureaucracies (researchers, administrators, extensionsists, etc.) without reference to local needs or social-economic and ecological constraints.

The 'Bottom-up' Approach

This facilities a two ways flow of information from farmers to researchers, administrators, extensionists and vice-versa, where traditional knowledge of their own are utilized and blended with the external experts, knowledge of genetic engineering, soil conditions and successful techniques used elsewhere.

In this study, the information was collected by the farm women of different WSM. A detailed questioner (Attached) and a format (also attached) was used. On the basis of this first hand information by the women of WSM all data was collected and results were made. Lastly, the basic thing that the grass root level women's voice is the base of this study.

REFERENCES

1. Malcolm Adiseshiah, "Development as people: The Total approach," UNESCO, the second development decades II,
2. See Henry Maddick, *Democracy, Decentralization and Development* (Botany: Asia Publishing Co., 1963), pp. 9-30.
3. United Nations, decentralization for national and local development (New York: Division of Public Administration, Deptt. of Economics and Social Affairs, Sales No UN–Publication, 62. H.H., pp. 31.

2

Shiwalik Hills

The Shiwalik sediments of the western Himalaya extended from Jammu and Kashmir through, Haryana, Himachal Pradesh and Uttarakhand to Nepal for more than 1500km. The rocks are made up of stone, grits conglomerate, pseudo conglomerate, clay and silts having characteristics of fluviatile deposits of torrential streams. The Shiwalik group of rocks represents the accumulation of Neogene period (middle Miocene—lower Pleistocene). The sequence has been divided into the lower, the middle and the upper Shiwalik formations.

Medlcott (1864) was the first person who took up the geological investigations of the Shiwalik and associated rocks exposed between the rivers Ganges and Ravi. This way the first systematic study of the Siwalik group of Northwestern Himalayas. Middlemiss (1890) extended the geological investigations to hills of Garhwal and Kumaon. After this research work has been carried out by a number of workers but during past 60 to 70 years it has touched new heights.

The climate of Shiwalik is subtropical to sub-humid

and humid with warm summer and cold winter. Mean annual rainfall varies from 800 to 1400mm, bulk of which (about 80%) is received during monsoon. The mean annual soil temperature ranges from 15^{0}C to 22^{0}C and mean summer soil temperature ranges from 29^0 to 32^{0}C and mean winter. Soil temperature ranges from 8.4^0 to 15^{0}C. the soil moisture regimes are Ustic and Udic and soil temperature regime is dominantly thermic. Hyperthermic temperature regim [mean annual soil temperature >22^{0}C] is found in small areas adjacent to plains.

Moderately deep (50-75cm) soils occupy major area (64%) while deep soils (>75cm) and shallow soils (<50cm) cover 19 and 15% respectively. Deep soil can be used for growing climatically adopted cereal and oilseed crops along with plantation of fruit trees. Moderately deep soils on steep slopes require immediate ameliorative soil conservation measures. Plantation of khari, shishom, Babull, chir, siries, subabul, bamboo, with protective grazing should be encouraged to check soils erosion. Some improved fodder species should be introduced as part of silri-pastoral development. In addition, grasses like eulaliopsis binata, cenchrus ciliaaris, cenchrus setigerus, chrysopogon fulrus, dicanthium annualatumy stylosanthes hamala, chitoria ternaea etc. can be grown to meet the fodder and economic requirements of the inhabitants. It is not economically feasible to reclaim shallow soils, therefore, these soils can be put under forests as catchments for watershed development for animal husbandry and recreational purpose.

Majority of soil (67%) are loamy which included coarse and fine-loamy families followed by loamy-skeletal (28%), Sandy skeletal [1.0% and sandy (0.71%).

Loamy soils are cultivated for climatically adopted crops on terraced lands, while these utilized for plantation of fruit trees and forests. Skeletal and sandy soils should be brought under permanent vegetative cover of grasses and forests to reduce the soil erosion.

About 40 percent soil have steep slopes (>15%), 10% moderate slopes (8-15%). 17% gentle slopes (3-8%) and 25% very gentle slopes (1-3%). Lands having more than 8 percent slopes should be managed under silvi-pastoral and forestry development. Lands having 5-8 percent slopes are best suited for bench terraces.

About 36 percent area is affected by severe soil erosion, 49 percent by moderate and 13 percent by slight erosion. Stoniness covering 25 percent area is also the main problem in severely eroded areas. These areas should be treated by adopting suitable soil conservation measures to minimize the soil erosion losses. In this way we can say that shallow soil depth, severe to very severe erosion hazards, stoniness, storage, low available water capacity and low nutrient status, are the main construction. These soils need intensive soil conservation measures along with introduction of erosion resistant varieties of grasses, like 'Bhabber grass' which can also be utlilized for paper manufacturing. Some of these soils are well suited for raising horticultural crops, protected pastures, and forestry and recreational activities.

The principal source of groundwater recharge in the Shiwalik area is through rainfall. The area, particularly the recharge area, receives considerable amount of rainfall. However, the major part of the rainfall, goes either as runoff or evaporation and evapotranspiration. Only fraction of it may percolate to join the groundwater system. The rate of infiltration in this zone is considerably higher, due to course nature of sediments. The rivers and streams emerging from Shiwalik hills also form a signification recharge source. They bring a huge quantity of flood water during the monsoon season in the area. The other factors involved in the ground water recharge are inflow of groundwater from the adjoining areas, percolation from the surface water bodies like ponds and return flow from irrigation water.

As we know forests are important for maintaining ecological balance and preserving the life supporting system of the earth. They are essential for food for food production health and other aspects of human survival. In Shiwalik, there are very good and dense forests in the area. The main forest classes of the area are: (i) closed forests: it is an area within the notified forest boundaries where the vegetation density (crown cover) is 40 percent or above which accounts for 18366 hectare. In this category plants belonging to species Dalbergia sissoo, eucalyptus sp. Acacia Catechu, acacia mollissima, Acacia nilotica, Butea monosperma, prosophis cineraria, nilotica, na leucocephala, Bauhunia purpurea, are present. (ii) degraded forest: It is an area within the notified forest boundary where the vegetation density (crown cover) in below 10 percent. This category accounts for 0.11 percent of the total geographical area of Shiwalik. (iii) Block plantation: it is a area of man-made and or naturally growing tress of forestry as well as social importance raised/ grown on other than notified forest lands which accounts for 16575 hectares and mostly present near agricultural land, open field, roads etc. The most common species of plants present and Acacia sp. Dalbergia sissoo, prosopis sp, poplus sp, and eucalyptus sp. (iv) Strip plantation; strip plantation are mostly presently on the banks of canals, roads, railway lines and at times on the boundary demarcation of agricultural fields etc. it is about 5500 hectares. In this category, plants present mostly are ceucalyptus sp. Dalbergia sissoo, Acacia sp. Prosopis sp. and populus sp. etc.

The National Forest Policy, 1952 Emphasizes on protective functions of forest in maintaining ecological balance and environment stability, and aims to have a minimum of one third of the geographical area of the country under forest or tree cover. The policy enjoins maintaining two third of the area in hills under forest cover in order to prevent erosion and land degradation and to ensure the stability of the fragile eco-systems. It is, therefore, desirable to assess the extent of forest cover in the hill districts of the Shiwalik area. All the hills district under Shiwalik area have less than 66 percent.

People Oriented Policies and Forest

The first indication of forestry administration found in 300BC during Chandra Gupta Maurya's reign when a superintendent of forest was appointed to protect forests and wild life. The Muslim rule in India lead to the beginning of demarcation of land but a system of uniform forest classification was started for the first time with the advent of the British into India. In 1855 August, a memorandum of guidance restricting forest dwellers rights over forest was issued and later modified in 1894. The first forest act May 1865 Empowered the government to declare any land covered with trees brush wood, as government forest and to make rules regarding their management. But it was realized that forest were of different types and not every one had the same rights in forest land. As a result forest act 1878 divided forest into: (1) Reserve forest; (2) Protected forest; and (3) Village forest. A national forest policy was resolved on the 19th Oct. 1884. This act allowed the exploitation of forests for revenue. This underlined the basic premises of the Indian forest act of 1927. With modifications in this act, efforts were made to control shifting cultivation and the free use of timber as firewood.

The national forest policy resolution of 1952 advocated the division of all forests into three kinds (1) Protection forests, (2) Production forests and (3) Social forest. Social forests were given the lowest priority and the production forests the highest priority.

The Forest Conservation Act of 1980 transferred the issue of forest to the concurrent list. In 1988 central government announcement the new forest policy. The focus was on conservation of forest in place of revenue generation, with a view also to answering the subsistence needs of the communities. The main features of this policy were: (1) maintenance of environmental stability through restoration of ecological balance; (2) Preserving remaining natural forests; (3) Checking soil erosion and denudation in catchment areas; (4) Increasing forest/tree cover through afforestation; (5) Meeting the requirements of fuel wood, fodder and small timbers of locals; (6) increasing productivity of forests to meet essential needs on sustainable basis; (7) Efficient utilization of forest produce and maximizing substitution of wood; (8) creating massive people's movement to minimize pressure on existing forests. In June, 1990 the ministry of environment and forests, government of India issued the guidelines, concerning the involvement of village communities in the protection, development, management and regeneration of degraded forests, termed as 'Joint Forest Management' (JFM).

The policy document envisages that the voluntary agencies/NGOs may be associated as interface between state Forest departments and the local village communities for revival, restoration and development of degraded forests in this manner: (1) An agreement should be made between the voluntary agency/NGO, the village community (beneficiaries) and the state forest department; (2) No ownership or lease rights over the forest land should be given to the beneficiaries or any other agency; (3) Only beneficiaries should be entitled to a share in usufruct; (4) Access to forest land and usufruct through village institutions only and not to individuals; (5) If the beneficiaries protect forests, they may be given portion of the proceeds from the sale of trees when they mature; (6) It should be ensured that there is no grazing; (7) No agriculture should be permitted on forest land; (8) Cutting of trees should not be permitted before they are mature; (9) The benefit of people's participation should go to the village communities and not to commercial or other interests; and (10) If the beneficiaries and/or voluntary agency/NGO fails to neglect to protect the area from grazing and other interference, the usufruct benefits should be withdrawn without paying any compensation.

The Government of India has amended the guidelines for implementation of JFM. These amended guidelines are:

(1) All states should register JFM village committees under the societies registration act 1960, to give the legal backing. (2) Memorandum of understanding, with clearly defined roles and responsibilities for different works or areas should be assigned separately and signed between the state government and the committees (3) In certain states, community groups are already performing the essential functions of forest protection and regeneration which should be verified and registered as JFM committees (4) Dependency on forests should be the main criteria for allowing a JFM programme in an area. this programme will henceforth cover not just degraded forests but good forests (defined by crown density) as well. The treatment plans and MoUs will be different the two types. The guide lines issued by government of India. It has been suggested that committees should have a uniform name and that is JFM committees. The strategies for the JFM committees suggested are:

(1) Rainwater harvesting both surface and sub-surface, from the hilly areas and providing stored water for limited irrigation to the members of watershed committees. (2) Grass lease should be given to village societies only. The intermediaries be supplanted by village forest development societies. (3) Frequent meetings and workshops should be organised so that the villagers can freely express their views and perception and interact with forest functionaries. (4) Participation of women at all levels must be ensured. (5) Community should be effectively

involved in the preparation of micro-plans, implementation and monitoring. (6) Choice of species for plantation should be done in consultation with the village community. (7) Training of forest staff is must so that they are fully oriented with the concepts fully oriented with the concepts of JFM. (8) Forest officials and the community members should be taken to other successful projects where they can interact with their counterparts.

The guidelines on JFM issued by the government of India say, there is "immense potential" and 'genuine need' for women's participation in theirs programme. According to guidelines:

(1) Henceforth, at least 50 of committee general body have to be represented by women members; (2) At least 50% of women members should be present for any meeting; (3) At least of third of executive committee member should be women—the quorum for a meeting in this case will be a third of women members present or a minimum of one, whichever is more; and (4) One of the three posts—president, vice-president, secretary—should be held by a women.

3

Garhwal Hills

Garhwal region lies between Lat 29^0 26N-31^{0}28N and long 77^{0}49′E-80^{0}6′E with a total area of 29089 km^2. In the east the seagoing to separate fly the high hills of the Kumaun Himalaya forming district boundaries of Pithoragarh, Almora and Nainital. River Tons separates Garhwal and Himachal Pradesh in the west the snowclad peaks of the higher Himalaya make the Indo-Tibetan boundary in the north while in south this region starts from the foothill zone of the Himalaya. Administratively, the region embraces Uttarkashi, Chamoli, Rudraprayag, Tehri, Dehradun and Garhwal district of Uttarakhand. About 16.2 percent area of Uttarakhand is under perpetual snow which falls in the districts of Uttarkashi and Chamoli, the source region of the Ganga-Yamuna rivers.

The mountain system of Garhwal Himalaya has a north-west and south-easterly direction and can be regarded as a series of spurs from the Tibetan watershed. The geological history of the region reveals rocks of different character and different geological ages, ranging right from Archaean era to recent times.

The entire region of the Garhwal Himalaya may be divided into the following geographical sub-divisions:

1. Himadri (Greater Himalaya)

I. Himadri ranges

II. Himadri valleys

2. Himachal (Lesser Himalaya)

I. Himachal ranges and hills

II. Himachal valleys

3. Siwalik (Sub-Himalayan tract)

I. Duns

II. Siwalik ranges and valleys

III. Bhaber tract

The present land forms in the Himalaya show evidences of ice-sculpture resulting from the past gigantic glaciers. The glaciers of the present Garhwal Himalaya area; Alakapuri, Mandakini, Raikana, Kosa, Mana, Bamini, Nandadevi, Arwa and Khatling.

The Garhwal Himalaya serves as the perpetual reservoirs of water for most of the main rivers which are of immense value to the Northern India. The whole drainage system of the Garhwal Himalaya falls under the following systems:

1. The Ganga system
2. The Yamuna system
3. The Ramganga system

The whole Ganga system may be divided into three main sub-systems:

(I) The Alaknanda sub-system.

(II) The Bhagirathi sub-system.

(III) The Nayar sub-system.

The important tributaries of the Alaknanda sub-system are; Birahi Ganga, Mandakini,. Pindar river, Mandakini.

The Bhagirathi sub-system: The Bhagirathi originates from the Gomukh and after flowing for about 18km westwards, river Janhavi meets it at Bhaironghat. The uppermost tip-tributary of the Janhavi are Barigun Gad and Chor Gad. The Jalandhari Gad, Siya Gad and Pilang gad are main tributaries of the Bhagirathi between Harsil and Maeri. The Dhaneri, Nagun gad and Jalkur river are main tributaries between Dunda and Tehri.

The Bhiilanagana, the only sizeable tributary of the Bhagirathi, takes its origin from the Bharti Kantha in the northeastern part of the Tehri-district and joins the Bhagirathi at Ganeshprayag, near Tehri. The Balganga (Renamed as Balkhila) rising from the Shastratal is the main tributary of the Bhilangana which meets it at Pilakhi. Other tributaries are Dharamganga, Chonji gad, Nailchami gad, etc. the Bhilanagana system drains eastern part of Tehri district. The: Bhagirathi and the Bhilangana have formed deep and broad valleys with extensive river terraces like chham, Pilkhi, Chamiyala, Sirain etc.

The Nayar, consisting of two branches the western and the eastern Nayar, is a compact system of drainage which drains most parts of the Garhwal district. Both the rivers rise in the Dudhatoli rnage. The western nayar at first flows almost due north but soon turns to the west and southwest and after draining for about 77 km, finally reaches the junction at Bhatkoti, near Satpuli. The eastern nayar flows southwest as far as Kainyur, near Thalisain, then southwards till it reaches the border of Khatli Patti, then turns sharply to the west and northwest till it reaches the junction. Its total length is about 129km. After the confluence of these two rivers near Satpuli, the united stream then flows for about 32km in the northwestern till it reaches the junction. Its total length is about 129km. after confluence of these two rivers near Satpuli, the united stream then flows for about 32km in the northwestern direction and meets the Ganga near Vyasghat. The upper part of the Nayar valley is wide with thickly populated villages but the lower valley generally passes through steep hillsides and hence, less cultivated.

The Yamuna system: The western part of Uttarakashi district is drained by the Yamuna system (Yamuna-Tons basin). The Yamuna has its source in the Yamunotri glacier. After draining most of the part of Uttarakashi district, the Yamuna touches the western boundary of the Tehri district at village Bhatgaon. Here, it separates the Dehradun district from northwest. The Badri Gad and the Aglar Gad are the two important tributaries of Yamuna in Tehri district. In Tehri district only western parts of the Jaunpur block is drained by the Yamuna system.

The Ramganga system: A number of small streams originally from the Chorkhaldhar and the Khankarkhet ridges of the Dudhatoli range form the upper tip tributaries of the Ramganga. The mandal, largest Siwalik river of the eastern Garhwal, meets the

Ramganga at Loharchaur and a little below the Palain Nadi traversing through the Patalin dun, meets the Ramganga at Buksar. It enters the Bhabar area at Kalagarh and further drains the Bijnor district.

The drainage system in the Siwalik and the Bhabar region, lying in the southern part of the Garhwal region, reveals some salient characteristics. Except the Ganga and the Ramganga, almost all the rivers of this region dry up during summer and other dry periods. On the other hand, floods generally occur during monsoon period. Most of these rivers make high gradient hence, they come down at a very fast rate with huge loads of Siwalik debris. Here, they genrally inherit two major systems of drainage: (i) The Ganga system, convering the western part and (ii) The Ramganga system, draining the western part. The important rivers draining this part of the Garhwal region are—Rawasan Nadi, Sigaddi soti: The Badol sot and Regha Nala are two tip-tributaries of the sigaddi sot, Malin river, Sukha river and Khoh river etc.

The rainfall occurs in the hills almost throughout the year, though this amount is very less in some months.

Forest area: Garhwal Himalaya supports a wide diversity of forests dominated by Deodar, Chir, Kail, Spruce, Fir, Oaks, Sal, Haldu, Sisham, Khair, Sain, Sandan Sagaun, Kanju, Walnut/Akhrot, Thuner,Toona/ Tun, Bhojpatra, Pangar, Hayfal/Kanjal etc along different altitudes and ecological environments.

Forest provided a large number of commodities are used as raw material in industries. Most of the items obtained from forests are primary products which are to be processed to obtain final product in a consumable form. Wood is obtained from forest in several forms and for a variety of uses. It is taken out as large logs or round timber to given the shape of sleepers for railways, construction of houses, furniture and many other items. Trees are lopped for fuel wood and leaf fodder. There are over 3000 known species of economic plants and a good number of animal products. Medicinal plants, essential oils, waxes, starches, gums dyes, bamboo, cane, fibers, grasses, honey lac, fruits and vegetables are some of the useful items which are exploited from forest economically.

In Garhwal Himalaya, fuel wood is still the main source of energy for cooking, lighting, space heating and water boiling. It is especially imported for rural people as fuel wood is cheapest source of energy available to them. Fuel wood is regarded as a major forest produce in the region, as by volume, the wood extracted for fuel is more than wood extracted as timber. About 631kg. of fuelwood is consumed per person per year, irrespective of their socio-economic status. Winter periods require more fuelwood than summer season in Garhwal Himalaya. Most of the poor families use fuelwood also for lighting because of the paucity of kerosene and electricity. Low altitude populations expend relatively more energy for firewood collection, which is due to a shortage of fuel wood in lower Himalaya. Continuous consumption of fuelwood has caused serious deforestations in these hills. According to advisory board on energy, government of India, the requirement for firewood is of the order of 300-330mt as against 30-40mt of recordable production.

Forest Policy and People: preservation of forest is vital for health and economy of nations. India's existing systems of forest management are failing to sustain natural forest ecosystems, which is evident from the facts reported by Remote sensing agency that India also about 2-89% area of forest cover in matter of just 7 years, between 1975-82.

Evidences suggest that land and forest settlement procedures were introduced and an impersonal bureaucratic form of rule was organised in this Himalayan region, apparently in order to cater to the vested interests of colonial rule. During the 19th and 20th Centuries these operations caused widespread change in the nature of the traditional relationship between the human population and agricultural land, forests and livestock. Whether, it was the native king of Tehri State or the commissioner of Kumaon, both tried to gain control and domination over natural resources through administrative measures. The practical need to stabilize the tax system promoted the British at the outset of colonial rule to introduce a concept of the modern form of private ownership of landed property in India. Accordingly, in the Himalayan region the requirements of commercial capitalism forced the state, to invoke and asserts the dormant "proprietary claims" on forest resources in its favour and to usurp the traditional prescriptive rights of the rural communities. The private ownership rights over agriculture land tenure, which were traditionally owned by the native king, were granted to individual. These two conflicting trends of ownership of prescriptive rights on forest resources and the granting of the proprietary tenure on agriculture land had reaching consequences.

Gradually, as the rights of local people to use the forest products were curved by the states in favour of the government and private contractors, strong protest started coming up. The most sustainable opposition to government came in the hills. In Kumaon and Garhwal division, social protests were aimed directly at the colonial state itself, and the agitation reached its zenith in the summer to burn forest controlled by the government virtually paralyzed the administration. This forced the government to appoint the Kumaon Forest Grievance Committee (KFGC), in 1921 on the basis of whose recommendations the state government reclassified the forests, transferred about 4500 km^2 of forests into the control over revenue authorities and, what is more important, lopping and grazing rules were relaxed except in regeneration areas. The report of the committee appointed in 1921 was known as the 'Forest Grievance committee Report'. The grievances which were brought to the notice of the committee were as follows: (1) Demarcation, owing to which forest boundary pillars often came too close to cultivation or buildings (2) Lopping restrictions. (3) Restrictions on grazing. (4) Employment of forest guards to enforce numerous rules and regulations and their constant interference with women and children, who under the custom in vogue in the hills are the chief people who on behalf of the villagers exercise such rights as of lopping, collection of minor produce, grazing etc. (5) Large number of forest cases which have either to be compounded or fought out in a criminal court. (6) Unsatisfactory methods of dealing with indents for timber. (7) Rules regarding fire protection. (8) Measured land was taken up within the reserves and in some cases in adequate or nc compensation was given. (9) Prohibition of all extension of cultivation within the reserves. Pt. Govind Ballabh Pant in his book "The Forest Problem" in Kumaon,

(1922) suggested that: (i) Every possible facility should be given to the villagers to obtain fire arms for the protection of their crops and lives. Not only had this shall the government make a special grant to advance loan to the villagers to enable them to purchase fire arms. (ii)These should be no restriction whatsoever in the matter of shooting etc in the protected or reserved forest. Every individual holding an arms license should be entitled to shoot. In case of forests lying outside the village the village boundaries, there should be no restriction in the matter of the removal of minor forest produce, and the restrictions should be confirmed only to some species of timber etc.

On the same time the Kumaon Grievances committee reclassified the forest into 2 categories—Class I and Class II forests. The class I forests were placed under the direct control of the District Magistrate and chief restrictions in these forests were: (1) No protected tree to be felled without the permission on the authorities concerned. (2) In demarcated area, no cultivation be permitted. (3) No forest produce be sold except for meeting the needs of he village artisans and craftsman. The class II forest were placed under the control of the forest department and the general object of the management in these forests were: (1) To provide for the requirement of the right holders, (2) to obtain resin and timber from Chir and fuel and charcoal from oak forests, (3) to improve the quality and density of forests and to obtain regeneration to the normal extent, and (4) to protect hill tracts from erosion and to preserve water resources.

The Kumaon grievance committee also recommended that the forest left for villagers should be placed under the Panchayats. The basic purpose of the Forest Grievances Committee was to given a free hand to the villagers as regards felling of trees by transferring the control of class I forest to the revenue department. Thus during the year 1924-25 and 1925-26, maximum deforestation took place. It was sheer blunder on the part of the grievances committee and Pt. G.B. Pant to advocate indiscriminate felling of trees in class I forest. For a moment it quelled the resentment of the people but its negative effects were felt afterwards and class I forests started deteriorating very rapidly owning to lack of protection, which resulted in mal treatment and over felling. After independence, the government orders were issued again for the transference of class I forests to the forest department.

In 1981, Garhwal Himalayas per captia cultivated land availability decreased from 0.174 to 0.095 ha. The per capita forest area during the same time decreased from 1.28ha to 0.77ha.

An accurate assessment of the forest cover in Garhwal is rather difficult partly because of complex topography and partly on account of administrative and soil factors. In spite of successive land settlements, there still are benap or unmeasured lands. Likewise, the areas of civil forests and Panchyati forests are not demarcated on maps and again it is not exactly known how much of such areas have been encroached upon for agriculture and other uses. Historically, the people had unlimited rights over forest and forest produce. Extension of cultivation on Nayabad grant lands was being regularised till recently. All these factors make it difficult to assess the actual area under forests.

Forest ownership: various systems of forest ownership and management existed during different phased of history and even in contemporary context considerably different principals and practice are popular in different part of the world. In context of Garhwal, out of the total recorded forest area of 22,911km^2 the forest department manages about 17,275km^2, civil and soyam forests account for 4,386km^2 and Van Panchyats forests for 868km^2. van Panchayats are only in Pauri and Chamoli districts. The ownership of the forests of Uttarakhand falls in the following three categories: (1) Reserve forest under the state forest department (2) civil and soyam forests under the revenue department; and (3) van Panchayats under local elected Panchayats.

By and large the forests under the state forests development are protected and better managed along the sound silvicultural practices. But there are some problems like: (1) No regular plans were prepared for rejuvenation or plantation of these areas. (2) No investments were made in these forests. Even the income from these areas was not generally ploughed back to protect or enhance productivity of these areas. (3) The staff for these areas is neither properly trained not adequate in strength, (4) the supervision, both technical and administrative is nominated as revenue authorities have neither the time nor the inclination to oversee them. Now some areas have been handed over to social forestry divisions under forest department, (5) Chunks of these areas have been diverted to agriculture and other non-forestry activities by villagers and revenue authorities. (6) Most of these areas are in scattered patches of less than 5ha which increased protection and supervision consts and (7) these area are treated as 'no man's land' and there is no visible authority to check their misuse or stop encroachments thereon. People have almost unlimited rights on these forests.

Management conflicts of forests: hills of Uttarakhand are environmentally perhaps the most degraded mountainous areas in the world. Increasing pressure of growing human and animal population also accelerated the pace of degradation and denudation of the hills. Consequently the hills are bardly productive enough to provide even the subsistence needs of the people and their animals. All the natural "common property resources" in the hills suffer from the "Tragedy of the commons." They are: (1) The tension between the forest and the local people is continue. The human and cattle populations have increased but the allotment of the wood and timber is on the basis of last forest settlement undertaken several decades ago. The forest policy after the forties mainly concentrated on commercialisation of forests with the result that new commercial tree species planted were not of much use to villagers either as fodder or as fuel. The system of contractors in forests managements also played havoc. As the demand outstrip the supply or availability tensions builds up, people would like that the first charge on the forest produce should be their. In these circumstances, especially in the interior hills areas, people have no alternative but meet their fuel, fodder and timber requirements from the local forest resources. They have no money to purchase them and even with existing concessions, women have to collect fuel and fodder almost on daily basis from distant areas as forests are not available in the vicinity. (2) On the other hand forester thinks that local people are inimical to forests and do not allow proper protection and conservation. Often forest fires are attributed to local people. The people perceive forests as an integral part of their being would like such forest species which are beneficial to them so that their requirements are met. This dichotomy stands between the forest Deptt. personnel and the hill people. This reciprocal hostility has given rise to the well known CHIPKO movement in Uttarakhand. (3) Conflicts with neighbouring villages are common, especially since they are the most common antagonists involved in pilferage from the Panchayati forests. (4) There is inequity in availability of timber since the royalty charged is fairly high and only the richer section can efford it. (5) Most of the persons agree that the illegal encroachment on forestland as a major problem is erated by Mafia and land hungry people. (6) Biotic pressures has caused forest reductions all over the hills. The major problems has always been removal of trees to meet the domestic needs of the local people who view the forests as yet another gift of nature, like sunlight and water. First and grazing have also contributed to degeneration. (7) Disappearance of tree cover from civil and soyam lands was because of such lands being treated as open access lands, which were not managed or protected by either the government or community. on the other hand, both reserved and Panchayati forest could be saved from total denudation because of clarity on "who owned the trees. Conflict between short term trees. (8) Conflict between short term and long term interest of the individual as well as between the individuals and the group can not be resolved by the individual alone, as there are other individuals on whose behaviour he has little control. The local Panchayats could perform this function, provided they are strengthened and trusted with funds. (9) Stocking even state forests is poor. In other forests, namely, civil soyam, Panchayat forests, it is generally deplorable. (10) Yield of major and minor forest produce per unit area are low due to poor tree quality faulty silvicultural practices and low levels of care. (11) There has been increasing pressure on treat growth from outside the forests to meet a variety of household and industrial consumption demands of growing populations. (12) Use of forest lands for agriculture, new or expanding, human settlements, river valley projects, industrial projects or township, road land for other development projects has led to diversion of forest lands to non-forest uses with adverse impacts on environment and ecology. (13) The policies of the state forest developments are perceived as non-friendly by the local people. A gradual change in the orientation of the government forest personnel has been initiated but it is much too slow and poorly undpoorly articulated as yet. (14) Forest administration is generally thinly distributed and is not action as well extension oriented. (15) Forestry is often treated in isolation from the overall problems of land management (16) Technology problems of land management are still inadequate and infrastructure in areas like communications, research, fire fighting, training etc. is insufficient. (17) People's specially women involvement in forest protection, forest management and the sharing of benefits from forest produce is yet to emerge in a substantial way. The concept of Joint Forest Management, accepted in principle by the government of India as far back as 1990, has yet to find fruition in the region of the country.

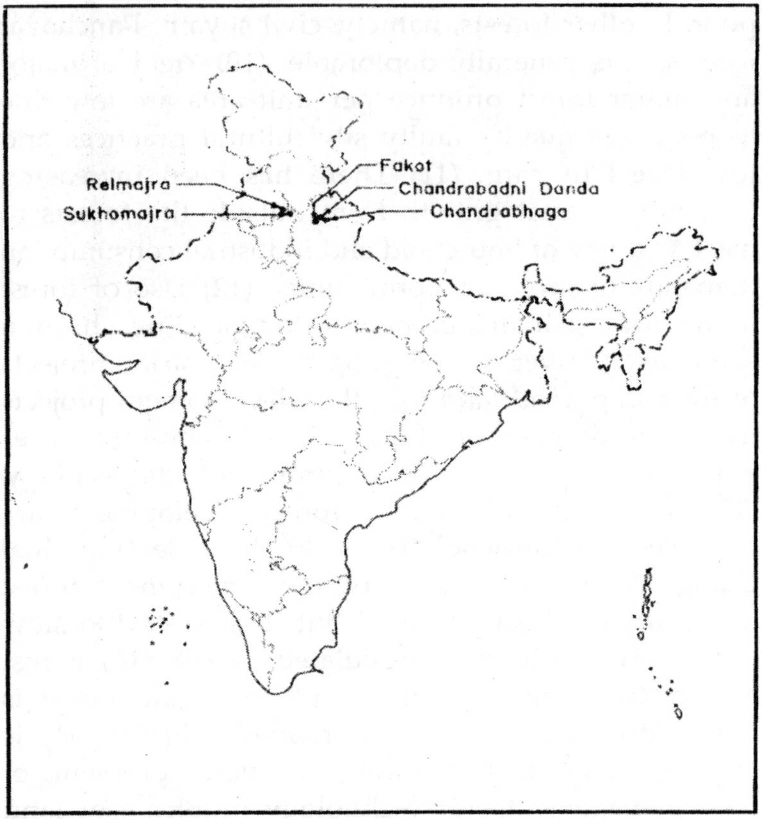

Fig. 1. Location Map of study area of watersheds

4

Introduction to Different Watershed Management

1. Sukhomajri WSM

The Sukhomajri WSM project, which has been acclaimed nationally and internationally as a model is Basically the contribution of the team of experts of CSWCRTI, Chandigarh Forest Department (FD), Haryana. The concept of WSM in the context of Sukhomajri has been defined as "the integration of technologies within the boundaries of drainage system for optimum development of land, water and plant resources accoding to meet the minimum needs of people." (Mittal, S.P. 1996, pp. 218). This approach according to Mr. Mittal has paved at the way for integrating the existing technologies for land treatment, soil and water conservation, afforstation, augmentation and development of water resources and increasing crop and animal production, to ultimately improve at the socio-economic conditions of an area in holistic manner. People's participation is WSM planning and implementation is considered as vital and crucial (Please see Fig. 2).

Shiwalik hills of northern-west states of Haryana, Himachal Pradesh, Jammu and Kashmir, Punjab and Uttaranchal are perhaps the most degraded hilly system in the country. Due to heavy biotic pressure (uncontrolled, grazing and reckless removal of vegetation) the dense forest gradually gave way to boulders, deep gullies and chasms. The problem became so serious that in highly grazed Shiwaliks often 4 to 6 cm of top soil would disappear with one heavy shower (Franda, 1981). Most of the rain water during monsoon (July through September) ended in runoff bringing with it huge boulders and betroths leading to the problem of soil erosion in Shiwalks can be realized from Sukhna lake of Chandigarh built in 1958. Within a period of 10 years of its creation, more than 65 percent of its capacity was filled with sediment coming from 4207 ha of catchement area. Out of 4207 ha, about 3214 ha lies in the Shiwalik hills. Till 1974 the average net sediment getting deposited in the lake was 14t/ha/year (Mishra et al, 1980).

The Operational Research Project Sukhomajri, Nada and Bunga demonstrated due possibilities of achieving conservation linked production goals from both farm and forest lands with people's participation through integrated watershed management approach as the state getting replicated in the adjoining areas. The HFD took the lead. In due foothill region of Punjab and Haryana state, 109 Sukhomajri type projects were completed by the end of 1990-91 at a total cost of 55.16 million rupees.

Details of Sukhomajri type watershed management

projects completed in Punjab and Haryana upto 1990-91:-

Table 1: Details of Sukhomajri Type Watershades

Name of State	*No. of Project completed*	*Area covered (ha) Catchment*	*Command*	*Total cost (Million Rs).*
Haryana	80	2303	3247	40.65
Punjab	29	817	752	14.51
Total	109	3120	3999	55.16

With the execution of these an area of 3120 ha of denuded forest catchment has received protection and 3999 ha of rainfed agricultural land in command have started producing sustainable crops due to the facility of supplemental irrigation. The average cost per hectare metre of storage (at 1988 prices) for 67 dams completed in Haryana between 1976 and 1988 was worked out to be Rs. 21684 and the average catchment and command area was 323 and 47ha. It is estimated that additional grain worth 1.8 million rupees, bhabbar grass worth 1.56 million rupees, forage grass worth 0.94 million rupees and other crops worth 0.8 million rupees are now being produced annually in the project villages. In addition, there is an increase of 5 to 7 times in growing tree stock in the forest area. The farmers have started taking interest in the protection of the forest after seeing the flow of visible benefits from the forests land. These projects primarily meant for mitigating poverty, resources starvation and social tensions, have benefited the farmers of those area which could not harness the benefits of development due to geographical limitations (S.S. Grewal, Samra, J.S. Mittal, S.P. and Agnihotri, Y., 1997).

Sukhomajri Village

Sukhomajri is a small hamlet located at Shiwalik foothills 30km. North-east of Chandigarh on Pinjore-Nalagarh road at 30.50′ latitude and 76.53′ longitude, in Panchkula district of Haryana in 1975, the village had no resource of irrigation. The entire agricultural land (52ha) was under rainfed single cropping. Small land holdings (less than one hectare per family) and frequent crop failures due to subsistence to the people. Each family was keeping large number of goats to eke out a living. Goats were allowed to graze freely in the nearly hills. Years of over grazing had made even toughest of shrubs and grazes scrawny. Villagers restored to illicit cutting of trees from hilly areas for fuelwood. Denudation in the surrounding hills was so fast that hill slopes once clothed with green cover were rendered totally nabbed. Not even a blade of grass was to be seen. Sheer needs of substance forced the poor villagers to decimate the very base of their survival. Today Sukhomajri emerged as participation, as a important component of sustainable development of WSM. Without this concept, it is difficult to achieve the goal of 'Integrated WSM. Suppose, we are not able to achieve this goal at least we can understand the causes of gaps behind the concept and also can evolve this concept for future watershed management.

Profile of Sukhomajri Village and WSM

Village Name	*Sukhomajri*
Total No. of families	119
Total population	720
Women population	178
Av. Family size	6.07
Literacy rate	55%

Public facilities	*Public Facilities*
Primary School	1
Anganwadi	1
Dharamshala	1
Private shops	5
Temple	1

Public facilities are required according the women on priority basis:

A. Sub-health centre

B. Primary health centre

C. Veterinary centre

D. Secondary & High Schools

E. Adult Education centre

F. Co-operative Bank and shop

G. Rural Bank

Table 2: Details of Rainwater Harvesting Projects in and Around Sukhomajri

Name	*Year of*	*Catchment construction*	*Storage area (ha)*	*Command capacity*	*(Cost Rs.) area (ha) (m³)*
Sukhomajri I	1976	4.3	8,000	6.0	72,000
Sukhomajri II	1978	9.2	55,600	20.0	1,09,000
Sukhomajri III	1980	1.5	9,500	2.0	23,000
Sukhomajri IV	1985	2.6	19,300	5.0	1,50,000
Total		17.6	92,400	33.0	3,54,000

Relmajri WSM

The project area is located in village Relmajri, district, Ropar (latitude 31⁰N, longitude 76⁰28′E) at an elevation of 280 m above mean sea level (please see the Fig.3). This village is situated at the Shiwalik foothills, about 9km. North from Ropar on Ropar-Hoshiarpur road. The watershed drains into river Satluj. There are six namely Bara Chor, Chitkar, Sukla, Badholi, gufanwala

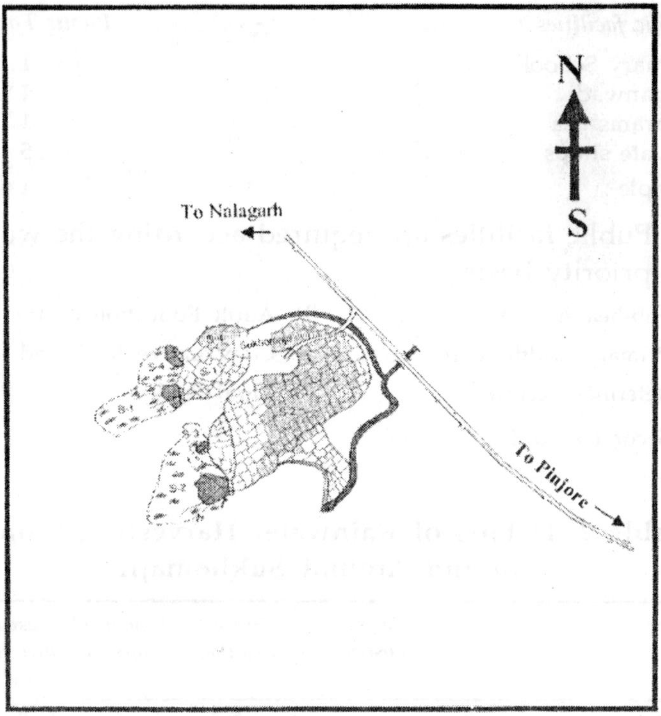

Fig. 2. Sukhomajri watershed

and Khol, which carry the runoff water from six independent sub-catchments.

How this watershed is different and important: In comparison to Sukhomajri this village is a big village with heterogeneous society. The state of Punjab in comparison to Haryana having different laws and way to manage natural resources. In this village near about 13 communities are living including S.C., S.T. those who are mostly landless. In this manner this is the village which represents Indian problems related to Indian society in a appropriate manner. On the other hand in Sukhomajri there is only one community and one cast people have less representation of Indian society and problems.

Profile of Relmajra

Profile of Village Selected Under Relmajri

Status	*Number*
Total No. of village	1
Total No. of family	42
Total population	336
Women population	144
Average family size	8.0
Literacy Rate	61%

Public Facilities:

Public facilities	*Number*
Primary School	1
High School	1
Community Centre	1
Dharamshala	1
Primary Health Centre	1
Private shop	1
Temple	1
Dispensary	1
Post office	1
Punjab National Bank	1
Co-operative society	1
Milk Dairy	1

Public facilities are required:

Public facilities
A. Sub health Centre
B. Primary
C. Veterinary Centre
D. Adult Education Centre
E. Rural Bank
F. Nursery

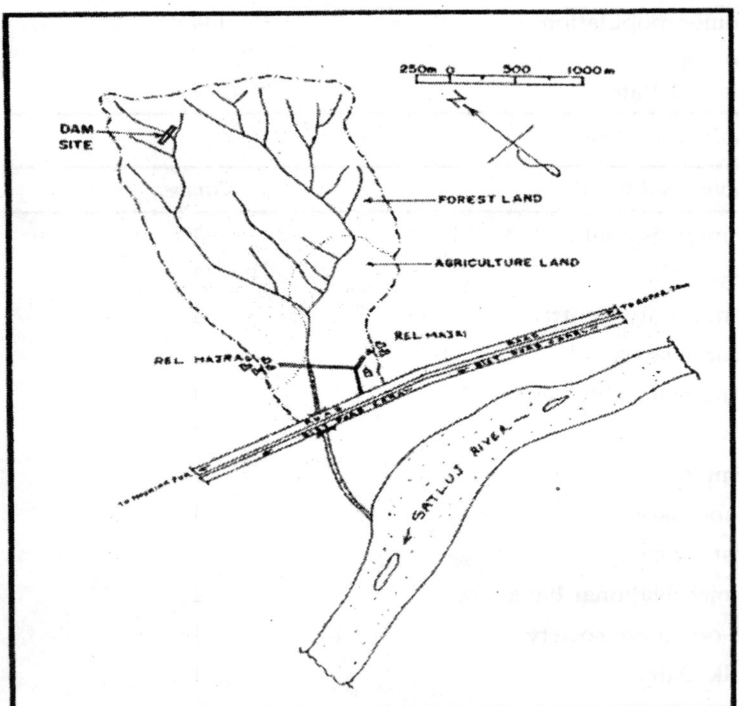

Fig. 3. Project area of Relmajra

Chandrabadni and Danda Watersheds

Chandrabadni and Danda watersheds are located in the proximity of Devprayag the confluence of the Alaknanda and Bhagirathi (please see Fig. 4) these watershed support 534 families (408 in Chandrabadni watershed and 126 familities in Danda watershed). These families are spread over 18 villages (11 in Chandrabadni Watershed and 7 in Danda watershed).

BMA/PLAN decided to lunch watershed rejuvenation programme during July 1999 with the following objectives:

- To promote sustainable economic development of the communities which are directly indirectly dependent in the watershed?
- To encourage restoration of ecological balance in the villages.
- Stressing upon improving socio-economic condition of poor and disadvantaged section of the community especially women.
- Broadly, the watersheds can be divided into three altitudinal classes. The power slopes located between 600-1000m. This zonation is amply manifested in the distribution of floristic composition. The lower slopes are dominated by broad leaf mixed pines, this is followed by pine mixed oak where as the upper slopes are dominated by oak and deodar forest. Visually, the slopes facing the sheltered location from the solar radiation are having better forest cover compared to the one which are south or southwest facing. For example, Chandrabadni watershed has relatively better forest cover

compare to the Danda watershed. There exist a direct relationship between the degree of forest cover and availability of water. Compare to Danda watershed, Chandrabadni watershed has better water resources.

Keeping in mind the objectives of the project following activities have been undertaken during the past years.

1. Afforestation and slope stabilization.
2. Rainwater harvesting.
3. Drinking water augmentation.
4. Facilitating irrigation
5. Village feeder roads.
6. Nursery development
7. Human resource development

Following is the Details of the Work Done

Activity	*No. of Village*
Trenching	4
Check Dam	3
Plantation	1
Retaining wall	3
Open well	2
Khal renovation	1
Tank repairing	1
Pipeline	1
Tank	1
Canal	2
Feeder road	6
Nursery	2

Profile of Village Selected Under Bhuvaneshwari Mahila Ashram

Status	*Number*
Total No. of village	18
Total No. of family	534
Total population	3000
Women population	1068
Average family size	5.62
Literacy Rate	54.83

Public Facilities

Public facilities	*Number*
Primary School	7
High School	-
Health Centre/dispensary	3
Aanganwari	4
Private shop	7
Temple	3
Post office	2

Public Facilities are Required

Status
Road
Drinking water
Hospital
High school
Co-operative bank
Rural Bank
Veterinary Hospital

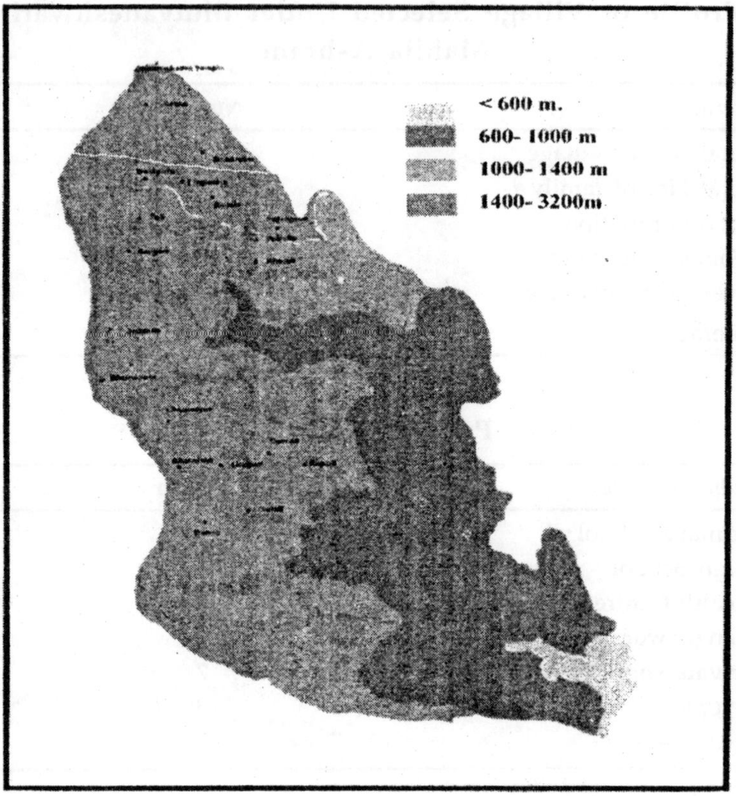

Fig. 4. Chandrabadni Danda Watershed

Chandrabhaga Watershed

Chandrabhaga micro-watershed of Risikesh Division–PVP: Chandrabhaga micro-watershed is situated between 78⁰14′35? to 78⁰19′48?E and 30⁰07′16?N, 30⁰15′16? Chandrabhaga micro-watershed is in Tehri-Garhwal district. Talani village of this watershed is situated in Narendra Nagar Tehsil of Tehri district 15km from Rishikesh on the road of Rishikesh to Tehri. It was selected purposively because women

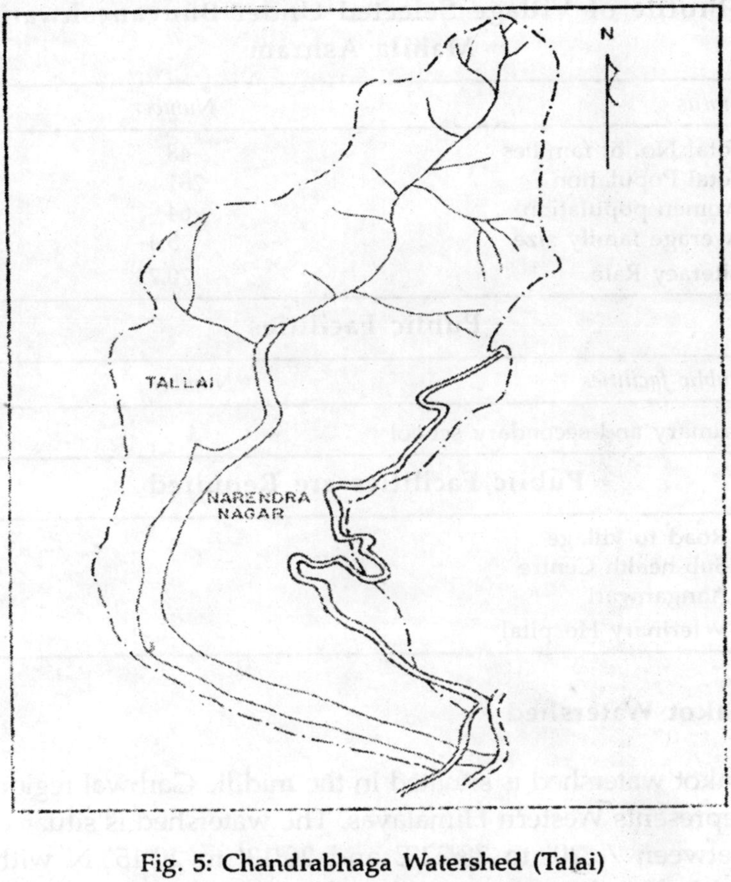

Fig. 5: Chandrabhaga Watershed (Talai)

participation in village level activities was high in comparison to other villages of Garhwal region (Please see Fig. 5).

Profile of Village Selected Under Bhuvaneshwari Mahila Ashram

Status	*Number*
Total No. of families	48
Total Population	261
Women population	64
Average family size	5.4
Literacy Rate	70.73

Public Facilities

Public facilities	*Number*
Primary and secondary school	1

Public Facilities are Required

- Road to village
- Sub-health Centre
- Aanganwari
- Veterinary Hospital

Fakot Watershed

Fakot watershed is situated in the middle Garhwal region represents Western Himalayas. The watershed is situated between 78^{0}20′ to 78^{0}22′E and 20^{0}13′ to 20^{0}15′ N with folded sedimentary rocks (Shale and stale). Fakot watershed is in Tehri Gahrwal district 50km from Rishikesh on the road of Rishikesh to Tehri. It was selected purposively as it has maximum severely degraded area (32.31) of the Garhwal region. The district represents ecological fragility, marginality, poor resource conditions, high risk and low pay farming situation. It is a typical watershed representing reserve forests, civil soyam, private and common property landuses and severe soil erosion problems. Moreover, the watershed elevation ranges between 650 to 2015m above msl in which maximum population of the region reside and therefore, have maximum biotic interaction with the natural Eco-system. The watershed drains into river Hiyul which is a tributary of major system of Uttarakhand hills i.e. the river Ganga. The important point considered in the selection of watershed was its demonstration value. The watershed is situated on Rishikesh Tehri higway which is the only important highway to connect the two districts namely Tehri and Uttrakashi, where maximum soil erosion problem exist. Pre-existence of Community Development Block near the watershed which provided necessary infrastructural facilities was another favourable point in selection watershed (please see Fig. 6).

Profile of Village Fakot

Status	*Number*
Total No. of village	1
Total No. of family	153
Total population	965
Women population	385
Average family size	7.8
Literacy Race	68.7%

Public Facilities

Public facilities	*Number*
Primary School	1
Block development off	1
High School	1
Cooperative society	1
Health Centre	1
V. Hospital	1
Aanganwari	1
Inter College	1
Private shop	6
Fair prices shop	1
Temple	1

Block Dev. Centre	1
Horticulture Deptt.	1
Medical store	2

Public Facilities are Required

- Road (within the village)
- Drinking water
- Seed Bank
- Compost pit
- Water storage tank

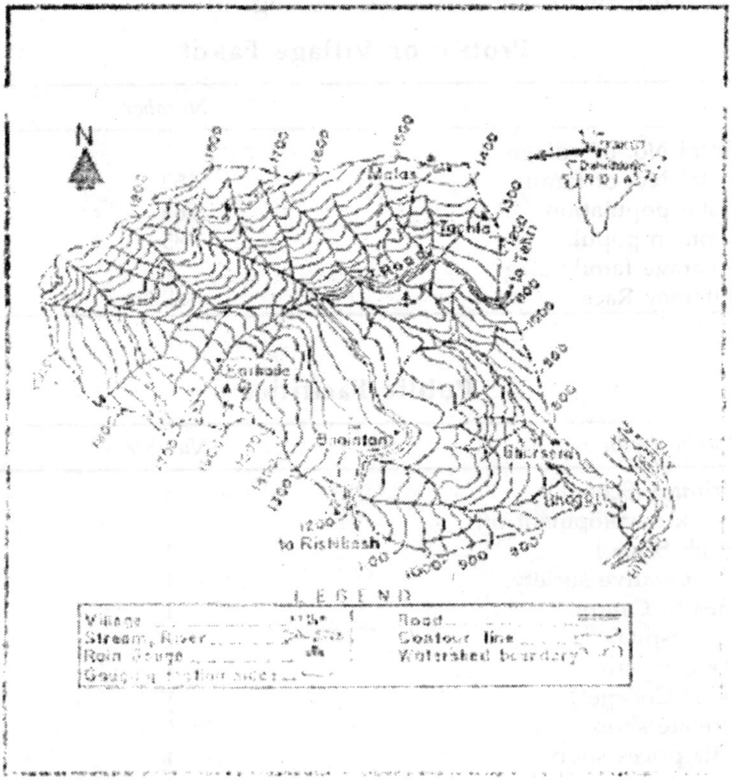

Fig. 6: Fakot watershed

5

Results and Discussions

Literacy

Article 45 of the directive principles of the constitution urges the state to provide free and compulsory education for all the children until they complete fourteen years of age. Not this article is going to become a fundamental right of Indian children (bill is in the Parliament)

Literacy and Education are reasonably good indicators of development in a society. Spread and diffusion of Literacy is generally associated with essential traits of today çivilization such as modernization, urbanization industrialization, communication and commerce. It forms àn important input in the overall development of individual enabling them to comprehend their social, political and cultural environment better and respond to it appropriately. Higher level of education and literacy head to a greater awareness and also contributes in improvement of economic conditions. It acts as a catalyst for social

Table 3: Profile of Watersheds

Watershed	*Sukhomajri*	*Rel Majra danda*	*Chandrabadni*	*Chandrabhaga*	*Fakot*
Year of starting the project	I 1975 II 1978 III 1980 IV 1985	1992	1998	1994	1974
Catchement area (ha)	4.3 9.2 1.5 2.6	59	-	-	15
Command area (ha)	6.0 20.0 2.0 5.0 3440	21.88	7356(map are) 3440	-	-

Storage capacity	8000	13.7	-	-	-
(m^3)	55600				
	9500				
	19300				
Total investment in Rs.	72000	2913230	-	-	50000
	109000				
	23000				
	150000				
Year of the with-drawal of the project	1981				
	-				
	-	-	-	1997	-
Project Name continue of	-	-	Continue	-	-

upliftment enhancing the returns on investments made in almost every aspect of development effort, be it population control, health, hygiene, environmental degradation control, empowerment of women and weaker sections of the society. Improved levels of literacy also are pre-requisites for acquiring various skills.

As for watershed programme is also one of the important development programmes and therefore there is a close relation between literacy and WSM. But it is very clear that pre-requisites of literacy are food security. No doubt that WS has given this security and people started thinking about education. As far as women are concerned in every WS literacy rate of people has increased. Bu still there is an urgent need of more education for women.

Mostly women in every watershed feel that their participation can increase only after getting good education. They have clear opinion that because of illiteracy or just literate, they cant participate at every level and only they can participate as a labour components.

Achievements at Present

Every child girl is going to school.

Problems

Higher education is still a problem for girls and mostly girls can't continue their education after 5th or 8th class in village.

Even today parents are not ready to admit their daughters outside the village for there education.

Table 4: Educational Status of Women Before & After Project (%)

Educational Level	WATERSHED									
	Sukhomajri		*Relmajra*		*Chandrabadni danda*		*Chandrabhaga*		*Fakot*	
	B.P.	*A.P.*	*B.P.*	*A.P.*	*B.P.*	*A.P.*	*B.P.*	*A.P.*	*B.P.*	*A.P.*
Literate	0	55	1.59	61.63	54.50	54.83	51.56	70.73	10.41	68.7
Illiterate	100	45	98.41	38.37	45.49	45.16	48.43	29.26	89.58	31.2

Because they think job opportunities are very low and after getting education these girls can't work in fields. In this way they create a new type of social problem.

Literacy rate increasing in all watersheds because food security and oveall socio-economy development has been achieved

Table 5: Literacy Rate According to 2001 Census (%)

National and State wise	*Total*	*Male*	*Female*
India	65.38	75.85	54.16
Punjab	69.95	75.63	63.55
Haryana	68.59	79.25	56.31
Uttaranchal	72.28	84.01	60.26

In comparison to India and state, Literacy rate of watershed is high because WSM area is rural areas literacy and census of 2001 has given combined % of rural and urban area.

Land

Land, particularly healthy soil is, is the foundation on which life depends. If the land is healthy then agriculture and pasturage will yield food in plenty. If it is not, the ecosystem will show signs of strains and food production will become more difficult. Because women are at the center of world food production producing more than 80 percent of the food in some countries any analysis of land resources must include an appreciation of their central role.

Even with the initiation of agrarian reforms, the politics of land ownership of the work ensure that the most productive land remains in the hands of a few. Where political power resides with a land owning elite, government allows private estates to expand and protect their boundaries.

In watershed area mostly farmers between .5 to 1.5 hac land. In Shiwalik region the land hodling is high in comparison to Garhwal Himalaya region. Major benefits are: irrigation has increased, food security have been achieved two crops.

Major problems are: Division of land within the family and only prominent people in the villages those who big lands are getting water from dam.

Landless Women and their Problem

In Rel Majra near about 200 families are S.C., S.T. and 99% are landless. 19 landless women interviewed and their views about the watershed are:

A) For them there is no meaning of watershed management for a landless family.

B) They have no right on water.

C) They have no right on forest because in Punjab JFM is not working and landless people have no rights on forest. This is called Mustarka Malban land mostly women were dissatisfied with such type of laws.

D) These landless people are depends on the fields of big farmer for labour and landless women are not getting equal money for equal work. Suppose if there is any caste conflict first of all big farmers deprived these landless women from work in their fields. In this situation the survival these community become a problem and they also use the wrong practices like stolling of grass and fuel wood from forest and from fields also.

E) Their representation is nil in HRMS. Till now they are not getting any water related work from watershed management.

Mustarka Malban Land (Punjab)

In Punjab, the JFM experiment is not initiated yet. One important and distinct feature in case of Punjab is that the major parts of the forest are belongs to the farming communities or it is owned privately. The forest protection committees (FPCS) are functioning only in villages having substantial forest area under Panchayat forest or Mustarka Malban land (common ownership of the forest lands restricted to the descendents of the original settles of the villages). In such villages interface relationship existed between the two institutions namely Panchayat and FPCs, which has helped in efficiently managing the forest and income from them. But FPC has absolutely no role to play in villages, where the entire forests are privately owned. So landless families in Shiwalik like Relmajra village who are mainly dependent on the forest based activities (especially rope making) have been in crisis due to (a) no-availability of Bhabbar grass in sufficient amount on cheap rate and (b) no share of the landless in the forest resources in this region. As per the guidelines of 1988 forest policy, the government of Punjab issued a circular in 1993 in order to provide ¼ share in non-timber forest produce to the landless poor like SCs and artisans, but the order were not implemented till now. Mostly landless working in the fields of landlords but whenever there is a conflict between the two classes first of all landlord people stop giving work to landless people in their fields. In these circumstances landless people faces very big problems and even sometimes they become the thief for grass and fuel. No micro plan has developed to involve the landless poor. Deep conflicts are also noticed between landless and farming community and court are also noticed against each other within the community.

Their suggestions are:

(A) Since centuries they have not given right on forest and land but in new situation atleast in watershed they should also be have some right on water as water is a natural resource. They can give their water to others those who are having their land or those who in need.

(B) Water related industries like fisheries and other should go to the landless women.

(C) For a just society these people should be involve from very beginning like planning to monitoring in WSM.

Table 6: Familywise Land Holding (%) in Different Watersheds

Land	*Water Shed*				
Distributors (in Hac.)	*Sukho-majri*	*Rel Majra*	*Chandrabadni Danda*	*Chandra Bhaga*	*Fakot Watershed*
Land Less	3.44	0	2.32	0	0
0-0.5	65.51	16	69.76	81.81	31.58
0.5-1.0	17.24	12	23.25	18.18	31.58
1.0-1.5	6.89	24	4.65	-	10.52
1.5-2.0	6.89	16	0	-	26.32
More than 2.0	0	32	0	-	0

Mostly farmers are between the .5 to 1 (ha) land

In Relmajra and in Sukhomajri land holding is high in comparison to Chandrabadni Danda, Chandrabhaga and Fakot watershed.

Major benefits are: Irrigation has increased, food security have been achieved through two corps.

Major problems are: Division of land within the family and only prominent people of village are getting water from dam. Other problems are mainly related to Chandrabadni, Chandrabadni and Fakot watersheds as described by women like: (1) Scattered and limited land holding; (2) low productivity as terraced farming is the only option; (3) lack of technical know-how and absence of local farm-related research; (4) absence of means of transportation; (5) Poor marketing avenues and poor finance; (6) Shortfall of labour due to migration; and (7) No storage facilities.

Suggestion from women of Garhwal hills are:

1. Chakbandi and Mukhalsar practices be abolished.

2. Rain water storage be made mandatory.
3. Mixed plantation be taken up in van panchayats.
4. Storage and gowdown facilities be extended in important centers.
5. Information dissemination about modern farming techniques and high yield variety of seeds be provided to farmers.
6. Traditional forming with modern inputs is taken up at a large scale.
7. Improvement in transportation facilities.
8. Bio fencing with local verities of Rambans be undertaken to ward of wild animals.

Dam irrigated land increased in Sukhomajri, Relmajra and Fakot watersheds but as Chandrabadni danda watershed is in initial stage and in Tehri village of Chandrabhaga watershed no scope for increase the land. In these area irrigation facilities have clearly seen through the Guhal system which has been converted in cemented Guhal.

Table 8: Land Irrigation Facilities in Rel Majri

Position of land	*(%)*
Agriculture land (ha)	79.1
Dam irrigated	27.86
Unirrigated land	73.14
Tube well/Canal irrigation	37.58
At higher elevation	1.83
Dryland	24.83
Flood damage	7.79

Table 7: Position of Land (ha)

Land	*WATERSHED*									
	Sukhomajri		*Rel Majra*		*Chandrabadni Danda*		*Chandrabhaga*		*Fakot*	
	B.P.	*A.P.*	*B.P.*	*A.P.*	*B.P.*	*A.P.*	*B.P.*	*A.P.*	*B.P.*	*A.P.*
Irrigated Land	-	98.83%	40.85%	71.07%	15.97%	15.97%	77.89%	77.89%	11.84%	25.60%
Unirrigated Land	100%	1.15%	59.15%	28.92%	84.02%	84.2%	22.10%	22.10%	88.16%	74.40%

Table 9: Land Position in Sukhomajri

Position of land	(%)
Dam irrigation/tubewell	53.72
Rainfed land	46.7

Time Utilization by Farm Women in a Day

Women participation is wsm regarding to agriculture, livestock and other activities can be observed very clearly that through project women are getting benefits in comparison to previous days when projects were not implemented. As a beneficiary of project her participation increasing in agriculture, livestock and decreasing work related to fodder collection, fuel collection and fetching the water. Entertainment and rest time is also increasing.

Reasons: Household activities related work reducing because of ready-made culture increasing in kitchen.

- Agriculture work increasing because now they are getting water for irrigation and getting two crops.
- Fodder collection work has reduced because of now they are growing and also purchasing from market only in rainy season they used to go to forest.
- Fuel collection reducing because maximum families are preparing dung cakes and also using LPG. In winter season they use to go to forest for fuel wood collection.

1. Household activities related work reducing.
2. Agriculture work increasing.

3. Fodder collection work has reduced.
4. Fuel collection reducing.
5. Rest time has increased in SM and RM watershed women though Garhwal Himalaya's women worked are still more in comparison to Shiwalik hills.

Being predominantly agricultural community majority population in Shiwalik and Garhwal Garhwal is engaged in agriculture and associated agro based cottage industry. The lesser and often outdated technological inputs virtually compel every member of family to participate in the process of production. Female members, traditionally contribute more in this regard. Thus since agriculture is the mainstay of hill people, the women have and are supposed to be deeply involved in it at all stages—preparing the fields, sowing reaping, harvesting and threshing to transporting and storing the grain. Further they have to look after the cattle and carry head loads of fodder, fuel, manure, flour and rock and clay in case of household construction work during harvest time they often to out to work after the evening meal and at times keep on working till date night.

In villages where potable water fodder or fuel is not available in closer vicinity, the women folk have to cover long distance to fetch the same. In such cases, their day which begins even before down is obviously much more busy and tiring. Those belonging to poorer families have also to work on the agricultural field of the better-off so as to earn bread and butter for the family, weaving, knitting and stitching for routine household needs and at times for economic reasons further tax their remaining free time, if any. Thus rural

Table 10: Time Utilization by Farm Women in a Day (Hours)

Activities	*WATERSHED*									
	Sukhomajri		*Rel Majra*		*Chandrabadni Danda*		*Chandra Bhaga*		*Fakot*	
	B.P.	*A.P.*	*B.P.*	*A.P.*	*B.P.*	*A.P.*	*B.P.*	*A.P.*	*B.P.*	*A.P.*
House hold including childcare	6.20	5.10	6.15	6.00	5.00	5.00	5.00	5.00	5.30	5.30
Agriculture/ Horticulture	1.10	2.10	1.15	2.00	2.40	2.20	3.00	3.30	2.45	3.45
Livestock	2.10	2.30	2.00	2.30	2.30	2.30	2.30	3.00	2.15	2.30
Fodder collection	1.10	0.30	1.30	0.30	2.30	2.30	2.30	1.00	2.30	1.00
Fuel collection	2.30	0.30	2.30	0.30	2.00	2.00	2.00	1.00	2.00	1.00
Fetching water	2.10	1.10	2.00	2.00	1.30	1.30	1.00	0.30	1.30	1.00
Entertainment	0.30	1.00	0.30	1.00	0.30	0.30	1.00	2.00	0.30	1.15
Rest	8.00	11.00	8.00	9.30	7.20	7.40	7.00	8.00	7.00	8.00

women folks may have to work for almost 14 to 16 hours daily most of which, paradoxically, goes unaccounted and even unnoticed and naturally unappreciated.

Mostly women also facing the problem of deplorable condition of water (drinking water). Water is a daily requirement for drinking on an average Uttarakhand is facing a scarcity of 300 Ltr./day against the daily requirement of 400Ltr/day. Various factors are responsible for acute storage and they are: (1) Reduction of water table; (2) Increase in biotic pressure; (3) Poor water management of existing water resources; and (4) Failure policy preventing exploitation of water resources. Because of the above causes people are facing problems like: (1) Acute shortage of water (specially drinking water) being faced in the hills. (2) Poor quality potable of water (3) Spread of water borne diseases. (4) Fetching water daily two times by women is time killing also.

Suggestions are: (1) Launching of awareness programme for better management of water resources (2) Proper management of natural water resources springs, rivulets etc. (3) Change in the forest policy for better access to natural water resources (4) Three layered sources of water and catchments area. (5) Practices sloping terracing can prevent soil erosion (6) Practices such as contour bunding, gully plugging, Jute nettijng and construction of check dames be adopted (7) national water policy be examined in Light of traditional rights.

Agriculture

Although rural women have contributed a lot in the

growth of agriculture in India through various development programmes, yet these very programmes have stimulated their marginalization (Shiva, 1995; Mencher and Sardomoni 1982; Mies et at, 1983 Swarup and Rajpur, 1995). The reasons are manifold such as biological, cultural mechanical psychological/ mythological and administrative. The relationship between women, men and environment is structured by gender-differentiated roles, rights and responsibilities with respect to the use, management and ownership of natural resources. Without understanding this mechanism even environmental friendly efforts can result in increased pressure/exploitation of farmwomen. Since, it is women's activities that protect and conserve nature's boundary in forests and in agriculture in hilly ecosystem and through such conservation works she sustains human life through ensuring the availability of food, fodder and water, the destruction of the integrity for providing stable, perennial supplies of water for drinking and for irrigation and for providing the fertility directly as green manure or as organic matter cycled through farm animals. Women's agricultural work in regions like the Himalayas is largely worked in and with the forest and other natural resources, yet it is discounted both in forestry and in agriculture. (Bandhyopadhyay and Moench; 1985, Bhatti and Singh; 1987, Kaur, 1991)

Even though women play a predominant role in agriculture and bear a disproportionately higher burden of farm production, they have been almost completely marginalized from extension services, training and access to productive resources. More importantly however, it is the disproportionately low percentage of women workers in the agriculture extension system that prevents it from reaching women. This male dominated extension system tends to overlook women's role in agriculture and proves ineffective in providing technical information to women farmer.

The government has recently come out with a National Agricultural Policy. It is a long term policy for the next two decades. It's aims are to achieve a growth rate in excess of 4% per annum in the agriculture sector; growth that is based on efficient use of resources and conservance of our soil, water and bio-diversity, growth with equity i.e. growth which is widespread across regions and farmers; growth that is demand driven and caters to domestic markets and maximizes benefits from exports of agricultural products in the face of the challenges arising from economic liberalization and globalization with growth which is sustainable technologically, environmentally and economically (Chaitali Pal). The policy documents discusses the following themes—sustainable agriculture, food and nutrition generation and transfer of technology, inputs management incentives agriculture, investment in agriculture, institutional structure, risks management and management reforms. These are major concerns which require immediate attention on a priority basis (Chaitali Pal).

The female labour participation in agriculture in the villages include sowing, inter-culture, harvesting, threshing winnowing and post harvest operations. It was interesting to observe that after project the percentage contribution of farm women increased in agricultural activities. In Sukhomajri, Rel Majra and for some extend in Fakot and Chandrabhaga watershed multiple cropping systems have been adopted due to the facility of supplemental irrigation. As far as

Table 11: Time Utilization of Farm Women in Agriculture in a Day (Min)

Activities	WATERSHED									
	Sukhomajri		Rel Majra		Chandrabadni Danda		Chandrabhaga		Fakot	
	B.P.	A.P.	B.P.	A.P.	B.P.	A.P.	B.P.	A.P.	B.P.	A.P.
House hold	6.20	5.10	6.15	6.00	5.00	5.00	5.00	5.00	5.30	5.30
Culture operator	10	20	10	20	25	25	25	35	20	35
Irrigation	0	0	0	0	30	10	40	20	10	5
Sowing/ ploughing	15	20	20	25	15	15	20	20	25	35
Transplantation	15	25	10	15	15	15	10	15	20	30
Fertilizer	5	10	5	10	20	20	15	20	25	30
Weeding/ Harvesting	10	20	10	20	15	15	20	25	15	15
Bunding/ Threshing	5	10	10	15	30	30	30	45	25	35
Transport	10	25	10	15	10	10	20	30	25	40
Marketing	-	-	-	-	-	-	-	-	-	-

Overall agriculture work increasing (-)

In Garhwal Himalayas cimented Guhl system has decreased the work load of women (+)

Now, women spending less time in irrigation activities.

Table 12: Time Utilization by Farm Women in Horticulture in a Day at the time of Plantation (Min)

Activities	*WATERSHED*									
	Sukhomajri		*Rel Majra*		*Chandrabadni Danda*		*Chandrabhaga*		*Fakot*	
	B.P.	*A.P.*	*B.P.*	*A.P.*	*B.P.*	*A.P.*	*B.P.*	*A.P.*	*B.P.*	*A.P.*
House hold	6.20	5.10	6.15	6.00	5.00	5.00	5.00	5.00	5.30	5.30
Digging and filling of pits	-	-	-	15.00	-	-	Nil	30.00	Nil	40.00
Plantation	-	-	-	10.00	-	-	Nil	10.00	Nil	20.00
Watering	-	-	-	10.00	-	-	Nil	20.00	Nil	15.00
Use of fertilizer	-	-	-	-	-	-	Nil	20.00	Nil	30.00
Plant Protection measures	-	-	-	-	-	-	Nil	-	Nil	-
Collection of Horticulture produce	-	-	-	-	-	-	Nil	40.00	Nil	60.00
Storage	-	-	-	-	-	-	Nil	20.00	Nil	30.00
Preparation	-	-	-	-	-	-	Nil	40.00	Nil	60.00

- Horticulture activities are observed only in Rel Majra, Chandrabhaga and Fakot.
- Chandrabhaga and Fakot are an example to increase horticulture in Garhwal Himalayas.
- Relmajra was has shown that in Punjab Shiwalik the scope of Horticultre is high.
- In hill area of Garhwal, it is very difficult for women to carry horticulture produce from fields to road side.

Table 13: Time Utilization by Farm Women in Cash Crop in a Day at the Time of Plantation (Min)

Activities	WATERSHED									
	Sukhomajri		Rel Majra		Chandrabadni Danda		Chandrabhaga		Fakot	
	B.P.	A.P.	B.P.	A.P.	B.P.	A.P.	B.P.	A.P.	B.P.	A.P.
House hold	6.20	5.10	6.15	6.00	5.00	5.00	5.00	5.00	5.30	5.30
Land preparation	-	5*	-	5*	-	10	Nil	30.00	Nil	35.00
Plantation	-	10*	-	10*	-	10	Nil	15.00	Nil	30.00
Watering	-	5*	-	5*	-	-	Nil	10.00	Nil	15.00
Use of fertilizer	-	-	-	-	-	-	Nil	-	Nil	15.00
Use of insecticide and pesticide	-	-	-	-	-	-	Nil	-	Nil	05.00
Collection of cash crop	-	-	-	-	-	-	Nil	30.00	Nil	60.00
Storage	-	-	-	-	-	-	Nil	10.00	Nil	30.00
Marketing	-	-	-	-	-	-	Nil	30.00	Nil	60.00

- Only vegetables for their own use.
- Cash crop activities are only in Chandrabhaga and Fakot ws.
- In Fakot cash crop programme is very successful. In order watershed, this activity can be increased.

Chandrabadni watershed is concerned this watershed is in initial face and there is no change in agriculture activities of women. According to Mr. D.S. Rawat (SBMA), it is difficult in hill area to increase irrigation land because their primary effort is to provide drinking water in this area. In mostly villages in this area drinking water is a great problem. In mostly area agriculture totally depends on rains.

Implements play an important role in agriculture. In most parts of the Garhwal women and even Shiwalik women also use the traditional agricultural implements. In Garhwal region there is no change in implements since centuries, for example in Garhwal region the implements are used, are very traditional:

1. Plough: use for digging and splitting of the soil. It is pulled by a pair of ox. Ploughing is mostly done by men but women may also do it though only under compelling situations.
2. Sickle: used by women for cutting grass, paddy, wheat etc. made by local blacksmith. It is often called to be the companion of hill women.
3. Harrow *(Suhagi):* It is used in soil preparation for plantation.
4. Spade *(Pholla):* This implement is used for digging soil and in carrying out underground roots like potato, ginger, and turmeric.
5. Axe *(Kulari):* Axe is used to cut wood for fuel and other purpose.
6. *Dharanti:* Used in cropping pulses, wheat etc.
7. *Pathal:* used to harvest sugarcane and to cut other material which cannot be cut by Dharanti.

8. *Mongari:* Used in cropping like pulses, wheat etc.
9. *Dhadhsha:* used in cropping pulses, wheat etc. It is slightly different from mongari.

Barring plough all the above implements are mostly used by the women folks and are thus directly related to their 'convenience and performance'. In some cases, the poorer women folks even have to plough due to non-availability of ox.

Livestock

Livestock in India plays a multiple role in the village economy by providing products for consumption and sale such as milk products, meat and wood, drought energy in agricultural activities, domestic energy for cooking and manorial inputs for croplands. In fact, it is livestock that provides some degree of stability to the village economy during periods of drought. Shiva (1988) estimates that more than two thirds of the power requirements of Indian villages are met by about 80 million work animals. She further estimates that of the 700 million tones of manure exerted by Indian cattle every year, half is used as fuel (which would otherwise require 68 million tones of wood or 27 million tones of Kerosene) and the other half as fertilizer, with dun providing 38% by. weight and 17% by energy value of applied plant nutrients in India in 1975 (World Bank 1991). The scarcity of resources such as wood as Kerosene further emphasizes the crucial role played by livestock in the village economy.

As started earlier, women play a predominant role in livestock management and dairy production. They fetch for the livestock, feed and/or graze them, clean cattlesheds, collect and process dung and milk the animals. Dung is also composted and carried out to the fields by women. In deforested parts of the country where trees and other sources of cooking fuel are scarce, women prepare cooking fuel by mixing dung with twigs and crop residues.

Like most other activities, women's role in livestock management varies across class. Women of landless and small-peasant household perform all the activities just listed. Whereas women of medium farmer households perform tasks confined to the house, such as feeding and milking.

Outside jobs in such households are carried out by hired labour. Women of rich farmer households, on the other hand, perform mainly supervisory functions. It needs to be pointed out however that women's role in animal husbandry is significant not merely as a consequence of the number of tasks they perform, but also because of their traditional role in integrating agriculture with animal husbandry.

No doubt those animals are very useful in rural life. In comparison to Shiwalik region the animal resource has not been fully tapped in Uttarakhand. As a result the farmers have to contend with the diminishing quality of produce from the domesticated animals. The problems are: (1) poor quality of stock resulting from inbreeding. (2) absence of technical know how. (3) Poor quality of fodder. (4) Cross breeding for better varieties rarely carried (cross breed between local variety and Jersey cow). (5) Facility of veterinary hospitals missing in village.

Table 14: Time Utilization of Farm Women in Livestock Rearing Activities in a Day (Min)

Activities	*WATERSHED*									
	Sukhomajri		*Rel Majra*		*Chandrabadni Danda*		*Chandra Bhaga*		*Fakot*	
	B.P.	*A.P.*	*B.P.*	*A.P.*	*B.P.*	*A.P.*	*B.P.*	*A.P.*	*B.P.*	*A.P.*
House hold	6.20	5.10	6.15	6.00	5.00	5.00	5.00	5.00	5.30	5.30
Grazing	60	20	45	20	45	45	45	20	40	15
Chaffing of fodder	15	25	20	25	15	15	20	30	20	25
Cleaning the animal & Cattle sheds	10	15	10	20	30	30	20	30	25	30
Milking	15	30	15	30	20	20	20	35	15	25
Preparation of dung cake/dung related	15	30	20	30	25	25	25	35	20	30
Marketing of Milk	15	30	10	25	15	15	20	30	15	25

- Work related to grazing has reduced.
- Numbers of buffaloes are increasing. Grass problem is also increasing.
- Milk production is increasing (Sukhomajri and Relmajra)
- One family is holding 5 to 7 cattle (Sukhomajri and Relmajra)

Table 15: Cattle Population (%)

Particulars	*WATERSHED*				
	Sukhomajri	*Rel*	*Chandrabadni Majra*	*Chandra Danda*	*Fakot Bhaga*
Buffaloes	54.51	49.31	18.39	40	20.40
Cows	4.12	15.75	45.97	32.5	14.28
Calf	18.09	21.91	1.14	12.5	2.04
Bullocks	9.00	9.58	22.98	15.0	28.57
Goat & Sheep	14.28	3.42	11.49	-	34.69

Suggestions are: (1) Use of good varieties of milch causes. (2) Phasing out of bulls and Donkeys be used for carrying burden (3) improving quality of fodder (4) propagation of traditional system of medicine for treating minor ailments in animal (5) Rejuvenation of veterinary hospital (6) As compared to goats sheep be the preferred animal for domestication.

Number of sampling size: More than half of the families have been taken for the survey.

- Buffaloes are increasing (in Sukhomajri and Relmajra number of buffoloes are in very good number)
- Goats and sheeps are reducing
- Cows are in good number in Garhwal Himalayas.

Problems

- Veterinary doctors are not available
- There is no proper way in Garhwal village to go with Buffaloes to cities.
- Grass problem is in garhwal region is very high

- Bawani village of Chandrabhaga watershed is an excellent example where all Lentana has been replaced by Hatighas (Napier or Pennisetum pupareum).

Fuel

In many countries, forest form the basis of civilization, India of example became known as Army Sanskrit, or a forest culture, and forest based settlements produced the best scientific research and cultural writings. The chipko movement in India expresses the value of forests in songs:

What forests bring us?
Soil, water and clean air,
Soil, water and clean air,
The basis of our life.

For centuries women have gathered forest products. "The time spent in forests, gathering wood, has taught women the many uses of trees, including providing fibers for cloth, mat-making and basketry. Many trees are used as a source medical uses of various trees. For women, trees and forests are multifunctional Trees offer "fuel, food and fodder" the Three F's as women say. With so much pressure on the land, women have little choice but to use forests. As there are no alternatives, women must gather wood and other biomass for fuel wherever they can. The rarely collect trees, they to be only twigs, smaller branches and often dead local community development" or "social forestry". Thus "Foresters need to adopt a truly social vision of development".

If the poor are to be benefit from social forestry projects, they must be involved and they must share in the results of the projects. Women's participation is constrained in many ways: Competition for land problems over land tenure; lack of time left after domestic duties; cultural taboos and lack of familiarity with forestry. Moreover, women do not have institutional and organisational support, Legal restrictions, absence of legal entitlement to land, and the low priority given afforestation in the minds of local people have all hindered tree planting efforts. In the face of these obstacles, suggests FAO, "small discrete efforts building either upon skills and resource women already possess or a carefully staged, well defined inputs" prone to be most successful (FAO, 1983).

Now, the need of the time is that appropriate hill and household technology be introduced to lessen the women's daily drudgery. Women themselves must be involved in such innovations because they have valuable suggestions and solutions to offer. "Women have more discipline in carrying out any movement", says Gurti Devi "Women can take it till the end, men change their minds."

Fuel wood consumption decreasing because of 25% of dung is utilizing for dung-cake and on the same time LPG Kerosene oil are also in use.

In the winters wood consumption increasing:

- Through gobar gas plant wood consumption can be reduced and the time for preparing dung cake can be saved.
- In Sukhomajri and Relmajra mostly men go for fuel collection but in Chandrabadni danda,

Table 16: Women & Fuel Collection

Factor	WATERSHED									
	Sukhomajri		*Rel Majra*		*Chandrabadni Danda*		*Chandrabhaga*		*Fakot*	
	B.P.	*A.P.*	*B.P.*	*A.P.*	*B.P.*	*A.P.*	*B.P.*	*A.P.*	*B.P.*	*A.P.*
House hold	6.20	5.10	6.15	6.00	5.00	5.00	5.00	5.00	5.30	5.30
Fuel consumption/ day/family Frequency of women for collecting the fuel from forest (%)	5-7kg	1-2kg	6-7kg	2-3kg	8-10kg	8-10kg	9-10kg	3-4kg	9-10kg	5-6kg
Every day	100*	20*	92.06*	-	93.02%	93.02%	90.75%	25%	90%	45%
Once a Week	-	-	-	25**	-	-	-	-	-	-
Twice a Week	-	80*	7.94**	75**	6.97%	6.97%	9.25%	75%	10%	55%
Once a Month	-	-	-	-	-	-	-	-	-	-
Distance covered by No. of women for collecting Fuel from forest (%) Lessthan 2km.	-	80*	-	75**	-	-	-	100*	-	79.16%
2 to 4km.	50*	20*	-	25**	-	-	-	-	87.5%	20.84%
4 to 6km.	30*	-	84.12**	-	53.48%	53.48%	75%	-	12.5%	-
> 6km.	20*	-	15.87%	-	46.51%	46.51	25%	-	-	-

* Only for men

** Men and women both.

Chandrabhaga and Fakot watershed only women go for fuelwood collection.

Fodder

The availability of fodder for the animals is a primary concern in the livestock sector. In 1985, only about 57 percent of dry fodder and 27 percent of green fodder requirements were being met (Chambers et al 1989). Fodder has traditionally been available from different sources in different forms. In addition to permanent grazing lands, livestock grazes on government forest lands, village common land, uncultivable wastelands and fallow lands. Due to shortage of green fodder, crop residues such as rice and wheat straw make up a significant proportion of animal feed. Grazing on private lands after harvesting has also been common for under growth and crop residues. Additionally, a small proportion of livestock are fed on fodder crops that are cultivated on private lands.

Since it is women who are responsible for feeding and maintaining livestock, the task of collecting fodder is undertaken by them. Consequently the decline of common property resources and their reduced productivity has affected women disproportionately.

In addition to common lands, women get fodder from landlords in exchange for labour or collect grass and residues from their fallow lands and from other public lands.

Women's role: Despite the significant role played by women in livestock management and production (The 1985 *Dairy India Yearbook* estimate women's employment at 85% percent of the total employed in dairy production), women's control over livestock or its products negligible. Even though women handle most production aspects, men assume cooperative membership since it is they who are the legal owners of the livestock. It is estimated that only 14% of dairy cooperative membership consists of women (MOA 1991). Income accruing from dairy activities consequently remains in the control of men who also held of the paid jobs in the co-operatives. Moreover, women invariable do not have access to training in livestock management and dairying techniques which is available to men through the cooperative structure. This lowers the women's efficiency and reduces returns on investments as it is the women who handle most production aspects.

No doubt the dependency on forest decreasing directly but indirectly we depend on forest only:

> The forests are the backbone of hill economy. They fulfill basic needs of fuel, food and fodder and also are store house of biodiversity. But due to lopsided policies feeling of belongingness towards the forest is missing. This has led many problems specially in Garhwal region are like: (1) Absence of forest management policy based on the local aspirations and needs of the people (2) Local institutions like the van Panchayats have become nonexistent. (3) Dependency on forest directly or indirectly based fuel and fodder has prevented the search for alternatives sources of energy. (4) In the name of conservation forest authorities prevent villagers from collecting wood or draw water from forests but development activities like construction of roads or microhydel projects go unhindered.

Table 17: Dependency on Forest (%)

Dependence on Forest	*WATERSHED*									
	Sukhomajri		*Rel Majra*		*Chandrabadni Danda*		*Chandra Bhaga*		*Fakot*	
	B.P.	*A.P.*	*B.P.*	*A.P.*	*B.P.*	*A.P.*	*B.P.*	*A.P.*	*B.P.*	*A.P.*
Fodder	90	70	80	65	95	95	90	50	90	60
Fuel	90	65	80	60	95	95	80	40	90	50

(5) Previous forest wealth is being destroyed due to occurrence of forest fires. (6) Sense of belongingness among villagers for forests is decreasing. (7) Local organizations with considerable experience in forest matter not given a due important by the government and local administration. (8) Increasing number of useless animals in forests, also creating problems.

Suggestions: (1) Implementation, planning and management of any development activity should be people centric with local partnership especially of women. (2) Disseminate information and propagate the use of alternative source of energy. (3) Change in policy on use of minor forest produce. (4) A complete haul of the forest policy. (5) Policy of deeming large tracts of forests lands as national parks or sanctuaries be changed.

Income Per Day Per Family

In Relmajra and Sukhomajra income increasing in all earning activities like farming, dairying, sale of animal and grass and wage income/service. But on the same time population is also increasing and land decreasing within the family division. So for the mostly men of Sukhomajri and Relmajra are working on the bases of daily wages or joining services. In Relmajra men go to Rajasthan for Paledarri work (loading undloading work). Mostly people are also earning from cash crop and Horticulture. But in the Chandrabhaga watershed mostly men are working and sending money for their families. In this area of Garhwal region people doing agriculture but this agriculture for their daily meets and hardly fulfill for 4 to 8 months. In Chandrabhaga

Table 18: Women & Fodder Collection

Factor	*WATERSHED*									
	Sukhomajri		*Rel Majra*		*Chandrabadni Danda*		*Chandra Bhaga*		*Fakot*	
	B.P.	*A.P.*	*B.P.*	*A.P.*	*B.P.*	*A.P.*	*B.P.*	*A.P.*	*B.P.*	*A.P.*
Fodder consumption/ day/family	10-20kg	40-60kg	10-20kg	40-60kg	8-10kg	8-10kg	1-10kg	14-16kg	8-10kg	12-14kg
Frequency of women for collecting the fodder from forest (%)Every day	100*	30*	93**	25**	93.02%	93.02%	90.75%	20%	72.91%	62.5%
Once a Week	-	-	-	-	-	-	-	-	-	-
Twice a Week	-	75*	7.00**	75**	6.97%	6.97%	9.25%	80%	27.08%	37.5%
Once a Month	-	-	-	-	-	-	-	-	-	-
Distance covered by No. of women for collecting Fuel from forest (%)	-	80*	-	31.75*	-	-	-	80%	-	79.16%
Less than 2km. 2 to 4km.	50*	20*	79.36%	68.25%	-	-	-	20%	87.5%	20.84%
4 to 6km.	30*	-	20.63**	-	53.48%	53.48%	75%	-	12.5%	-
> 6km.	20*	-	-	-	46.51%	46.51%	25%	-	-	-

* Only Men

**Men & Women

Fodder consumption increasing

- Maximum families purchasing fodder like Turi (wheat straw) and also growing Bazara in their fields for animals.
- In the Relmajra and Suskhomajri grazing system has finished.
- Now-a-days in the month of May and summers women are not going to collect the fodder. Only in the months of July and August few women go to the forest otherwise in Haryana Punjab-men go to the forest for fodder collection.
- Now, the distance to go to the forest reduced from 4-6km. to 1-2km.

irrigation facilities are good and people getting for 8 to 12 months food from their agriculture. But in chandrabhaga watershed also mostly men are working outside in service and women working in the fields of villages.

The last decade human power has been eroded as they no longer exerts control over the natural resources especially in the context of Uttarakhand and the problems arising out of such a situation are manifold: (1) Large-scale migration of able bodied men (2) Women burdened with agriculture and forced to take up menial jobs (3) people voice not heard (4) policies and plans made from top i.e. centers of power which are not in the interest of Uttarakhand. (5) Race to control natural resources is begins and it is very fast. (6) Health problems and social evils begin to take shape. (7) Dismal health facilities.

Suggestions: (1) To end migration people faith in the system be restored through equitable distribution of natural resources. (2) Complete decentralization of natural resources be carried. (3) Since women have played a pivotal role in preservation of Uttarakhand they should be made partner in development programme. (4) Prime importance be given to education which ought to keep in mind the local conditions. (5) Development should be a long-term programme with participation of common man and women.

Table 19: Gross Income (Rs./day)

Activites	*WATERSHED*									
	Sukhomajri		*Rel Majra*		*Chandrabadni Danda*		*Chandrabhaga*		*Fakot*	
	B.P.	*A.P.*	*B.P.*	*A.P.*	*B.P.*	*A.P.*	*B.P.*	*A.P.*	*B.P.*	*A.P.*
Farming/horticulture/ Cash crop	2	9	3	10	-	-	2	8	2	14
Dairing	10	30	12	36	-	-	4	10	3	10
Sales of animal	3	8	3	9	-	-	-	-	3	7
Wages income + Service	20	35	25	40	20	40	35	60	30	60

- Income increasing in all activities. On the same time population is also increasing and land decreasing because of land division within the family.
- Mostly men in the village of Sukhomajri and Relmajra working on the basis of daily wages.
- In Rel majra men go to Rajasthan for Paladari work (loading-unloading).
- In Garhwal Himalayas mostly men working outside.

Table 20: Occupation of Men (%)

Occupation	*Watershed*				
	Sukhomajri	*Rel Majra*	*Chanrabadni*	*Chandra*	*Fakot*
Agriculture	3.17	-	11.63	3.75	5
Agriculture + Service	17.46	24	34.88	37.5	45
Agriculture + Business	7.94	8	6.97	16.25	5
Agriculture + Daily wages	71.42	68	46.51	42.5	45

Women Participation in WSM Planning Management and Monitoring

Women participate in WSM planning management and monitoring is very limited. This is the general opinion that because of social taboos, these women are not attending the public meeting but on the same time maximum women's opinion is that these meetings are nothing to do because ultimately elite class of village or powerful persons will take all benefits of development projects. Now main question is related to real participatory nature of meetings. Though women gave their suggestion to increase the participation of women in development programmes. According to them:

(A) There should be separate meetings of men and women (Sukhomajri and Relmajra women).

(B) Formation of separate women groups at the grass root level (Sukhomajri and Relmajra women).

(C) Development agencies should appoint women motivators for motivation of farm women.

From the watershed of Chandrabhaga and Chandrabadni, it is clear that they have women motivators and the ratio of women participation in meetings is high in comparison to Sukhomajri and Fakot watershed.

Resource Management Society and Women

The villagers of Rel majra and Sukhomajri also organised themselves into a Hill resource management society, under the societies Registration Act 1860. Since stored water is a common property resource, its proper distribution and management is imperative. The society has a set of written bye laws which can be amended, modified or changed by the general body as and when necessary. The head of every family, residing permanently in the village is eligible for membership of society if he/she abides by the rules and by-laws of he society.

Management Committee: The society annually, by simple majority, members and office-bearers, of the managing committee from amongst its own members. This includes president, secretary, Treasurer and five other members. There are 11 members in the managing committee.

Table 21: Women Participating in WSM Planning

Activities	*Women in response about activities (%)*				
	Sukhomajri Majra	*Rel danda*	*Chandrabadni bhaga*	*Chandra-*	*Fakot*
1 Talking to village women at the time of planning					
Occasionally	17.40%	42.85%	23.25%	18.75%	12%
Frequently	-	11.11%	39.53%	56.25%	-
Never	82.85%	46.03%	37.20%	25.00%	88%
2 Conducting meeting of women at the time of planning					
Many time	28.57%	3.17%	69.76%	56.25%	-
Thrice at the time of planning	-	31.74%	11.62%	-	-
Thrice at the time of programme	-	36.50%	-	-	-
Once	-	15.87%	11.62%	18.75%	58.33%
Never	71.57%	12.69%	6.97%	25.00%	41.66%
3 Training of women for W.S.M.					
One training programme	-	-	55.81%	40%	-
Two training programme	-	-	37.20%	60	-
No training programme	100%	100%	6.97%	-	100%
4 Film show for women					
One show	5%	10%	30%	15%	20%
Two show	10%	7%	70%	75%	15%
No show	85%	83%	-	10%	65%
5 Pre-survey of WSM and women consent					

They have some idea	74.28%	73.01%	83.72%	98%	62.5%
No idea of survey	11.42%	9.52%	9.30%	2%	25%
Do not know about survey	14.28%	17.46	6.97%	-	12.5%
6 Other	-	-	-	-	-

- Mostly women unknown to planning of ws.
- Training programme for women were conducted in Chandrabadni danda and Chandrabhaga wsm.
- Pre-survey of wsm mostly women have no idea.

The important responsibilities/functions of the HRMS includes:

1. Every members of the society shall be equally responsible for protection of the forest, the hills and the existing and subsequent social property and assets.
2. No members of the society shall allow his cattle to graze in the forest but when needed shall cut the grass from the specified area in the forest and stall feed his cattle.
3. The society shall equally distribute amongst its members the available water, grass and all other products from the hills. The distribution shall be done on a price fixed by the society. The money thus collected shall from the social revenue.
4. The society shall raise social nursery and do the planting in the hills and the adjoining land and on road sides and carry on fish rearing in the reservoirs.
5. The funds generated from the sale of water, grass, fruits, fuel, timber and fish etc. shall be

re-invested in the hills for the multiplication of the social revenue and for improving the soil productivity.

6. Every member of the society shall enjoy equal rights and responsibilities and if any dispute or difference of opinion arises amongst the members of the society, it shall be resolved by discussing it in a meeting of the general body.

Sukhomajri HRMS started initially with 59 families in the village in 1983 and all became members after paying membership fee Rs. 10/-. A family unit was defined as one sharing a common kitchen as this functioned as a decision making unit. During 1989 the membership increased to 70 and as on 1.1.97, the total membership was 125. Initially, there were only 2 widows as female members of the society. No provision was made at that time to give fixed or proportionate representation to female members. The other reason being that agricultural land in all these villages is exclusively in the name of male members. Later on, some of the females also became members to get the benefit of fodder grass from the forest.

At present mostly women are not aware about the activities of HRMS. After the withdrawal of project the situation is entirely different. All system has centralized in the hands of one or two person. Every women unknown to income and expenditure of HRMS. Now there is no meetings regularly and recorded maintains is very poor.

Table 23: Details of women participating in meetings held by various HMRS

Name of HRMS	*No. of meeting Held*		*Average No. of meeting held per annum*		*Meeting attended by Women*		*Proper Records Maintenance*	
	D.P.	W.P.	D.P.	W.P.	D.P.	W.P.	D.P.	W.P.
Sukhomajri	6	0	6	No.	2%	Nil	Yes	Parsially
Rel Majra	7	-	7	-	3%	Nil	Yes	Parsially

D.P. = During the project.

W.P. = Withdrawal of the project.

Table 22: Membership of HRMS Operating in Selected Village (%)

Village	*No. of Female*	*Caste wise female members*		*Land wise female members*	
		High class	*Low class*	*Big land holder*	*Small land holder*
Sukhomajri	14	14	NA	NA	NA
Rel Majra	13	13	0	NA	NA
Chandrabadni Danda	NA	NA	NA	NA	NA
Chandrabhaga	NA	NA	NA	NA	NA
Fakot	NA	NA	NA	NA	NA

Only in Relmajra and Sukhomajri ws HRMS existing. Overall women participation in all activities is very low. Hardly 1.12% women are aware about the HRMS.

Table 24: Awareness of Women About HRMS

Awareness	*% of women*
Not aware	11.62
Aware but concept is not clear	1.26
Aware	1.12
Others	No answers

Table 25: Women Awareness About Financial Activities of HRMS (Sukhomajri & Relmajra)

Factor	%	
	No Idea	*Some Idea*
Income		
Sale of Bhabar	100	0
Sale of Fodder	100	0
Sale of Grass	100	0
Water Charges	100	0
Fisheries	100	0
Expenditure		
Salary of Watchman	100	0

Formation of Mahila Mandal

The community development programme accorded an important role to the organisation of women, who constitute nearly 50 percent of our population, so that their enthusiastic participation in rural development was effectively ensured. These organizations of women, known as Mahila Mandals, came to be established in a phased manner in different states. The broad objectives of these mandals, as outlined in several documents were, (i) to help women to participate in development programmes; (2) to act as an agency for planning, developing and executing programme for women and children; (iii) to provide opportunities for discussing their needs and problems and share responsibilities with others according to their interests and abilities (iv) to help them understand their roles and responsibilities; (v) to foster group in the implementation of activities; (vi) to develop different kinds of activities for the common good; and (vii) to develop leadership among women.

As we know wsm programme is also a development programme and for the success of this programme women participation is a very important component. In study area, it has been observed that in three ws—Sukhomajri, Relmajri and Fakot there is no Mahila Mandal exist but in Chandrabhaga and Chandrabadni ws Mahila Mandal existing and for some extent women participation in meetings of Mahila mandal are existing watershed is also high. To involve women in development programme like wsm formation of mahila mandal village level certainly help to increase women involvement in ws programmes. The women of Rel majra and Sukhomajri also feel that formation of Mahila Mandals in their villages are very essential and without such type of organisation they feel handicapped themselves.

Recommendations: In order to critically assess the findings of the study through those who are actively associated with women's programmes, a fallow-up workshop on the study was organised at the institute from March 3-5, 1979 as in integral part of the total projects. The discussion in this workshop was largely based on the issues emerging out of the findings of the study. The main recommendations of the workshop was that—the objectives of the Mahila Mandals should be redesigned on the lines suggested by the working group on development of village level organizations of rural women.

Table 26: Mahila Mandal Exist

Watershed	*Status*
Sukhomajri Watershed	No.
Rel Majra Watershed	No.
Fakot Watershed	No.
Chandrabhaga Watershed	Yes.
Chandrabadni/Danda Watershed	Yes.

Only in Chandrabadni and Chandrabhaga watershed Mahila Mandal exist. In Sukhomajri, Relmajra and Fakot women handicapped because they have no women organisation in village. They feel formation of Mahila Mandal is essential but no body is taking initiative.

Table 27: Self-help Group

Watershed	*Status*
Sukhomajri Watershed	No.
Rel Majra Watershed	No.
Fakot Watershed	No.
Chandrabhaga Watershed	Yes.
Chandrabadni/Danda Watershed	In some villages

- Self help groups are giving strength to women.
- In Chandrabadni and Chandrabhaga self help groups existing
- Jakhand village of Chandrabadni ws is a an excellent example of self help group.
- If we want to emerge a grass root structure with women participation such type of groups are very essential.

Women participation is constrained in many aspects:

1. Competition for land.
2. Problems of land tenure.
3. Lack of time left after domestic and agriculture work.
4. Cultural taboos and lack of familiarity with forestry.
5. No institutional and organizational support.
6. An absence of legal entitlement of land.

Others (feelings of the farm women):

1. Women are not invited to the meetings.
2. The times of the meetings are not convenient for women.
3. Many time locations of the meeting are not convenient for women.
4. Inhibition of women.
5. Women think that nature of meeting is not real participatory but just they are only for the increasing the number of persons.
6. Illiteracy and lack of knowledge.

Training

Training is a dynamic and adaptable tool of interaction and a powerful means of bringing women into the development process. Special training can revive and strengthen traditional skills and build upon their enormous fund of indigenous knowledge, so transforming it into the capacity for action. Training can also help to eliminate women's isolation and build confidence.

Most existing training, unhappy, falls for short of these possibilities. Often the only training to which women have access is in the so-called "feminine" occupation of health, nutrition, sewing, handicrafts, childcare and home economics. They have to be helped to develop a capacity for income earning, to be trained in leadership, decision-making and in new technologies. Their participation in these areas is still insignificant compared with the training offered to men. "Perhaps the most flagrant and best known dualism occurs in rural agricultural training programmes in which women's meager access to training in no way reflects the overwhelming percentage of time that they spend in agricultural labour".

But the experience of this study is that attitudes towards the training of women will have to change, and that more resources and better coordination are needed.

Most environmental training programmes on soil regeneration, afforestation, energy saving, water management—still discriminate against women but there are important exceptions to this practice.

The center for Human Development and social change in Madras, for example, annually conducts highly successful eco-development camps for young people, especially women over ten days, the camp participants have lectures, discussions, film shows and tree-planting sessions. They visit other groups to see and learn about practical environmental action. Good training can benefit women as well as the environment. In the Indian tribal areas of Chotanagpur, poverty forces rural women into head loading fuel wood. This further exacerbates deforestation. The Xavier Institute of Social Service tries to address this problem by generating training projects which create alternative sources of income for women.

Strategies to Enhance Women Voice in WSM

1. There should be participatory micro-planning (initial PRAs) with the sex ratio of 40/60.
2. Introduction of development programme through different tools like—demonstrations, film show, poster exhibition and examples of already developed society, specifically for women and by the women.
3. Formation of separate women groups from grass root level according to problems and social and economic structure with special attention to weaker section of women and landless women.
4. Formation of local institution of women like Mahila Mandals and self help groups and HRMS.
5. Training programmes for women in watershed management by the women.
   - A. Specialized training for a group of women which will represent all the section of the society.
   - B. This group will give the training to all women of the village with the help of development agencies.
   - C. Increasing the women staff within the development agencies like ICAR for rural women training as it is very essential.
6. The strategy of appointing a women co-ordinator (Successful stories from Kenya, Bangladesh, India).

7. Building alliances with other grass-root institutions like committees of Panchayat etc. project activities.
8. Promoting federation of women's group.
9. Local knowledge of women to be utilized in the design and selection of the place and project activities
10. Co-ordination between the different government departments like education (NLM), family planning and health etc.
11. Women oriented technology is pre-requisite to participatory sustainability.
12. Social and technical strategies must be within the project.
13. Principles of equity, women participation through HRMS and the empathy of the outside experts and timely financial help through various funding agencies.
14. Minimization of conflicts within the society can benefit most of the families.
15. For development of the capacity for achieving participatory permanence the women staff must be in both technical skills and institutional arrangement should receive highest priority.
16. Gender Sensitization.

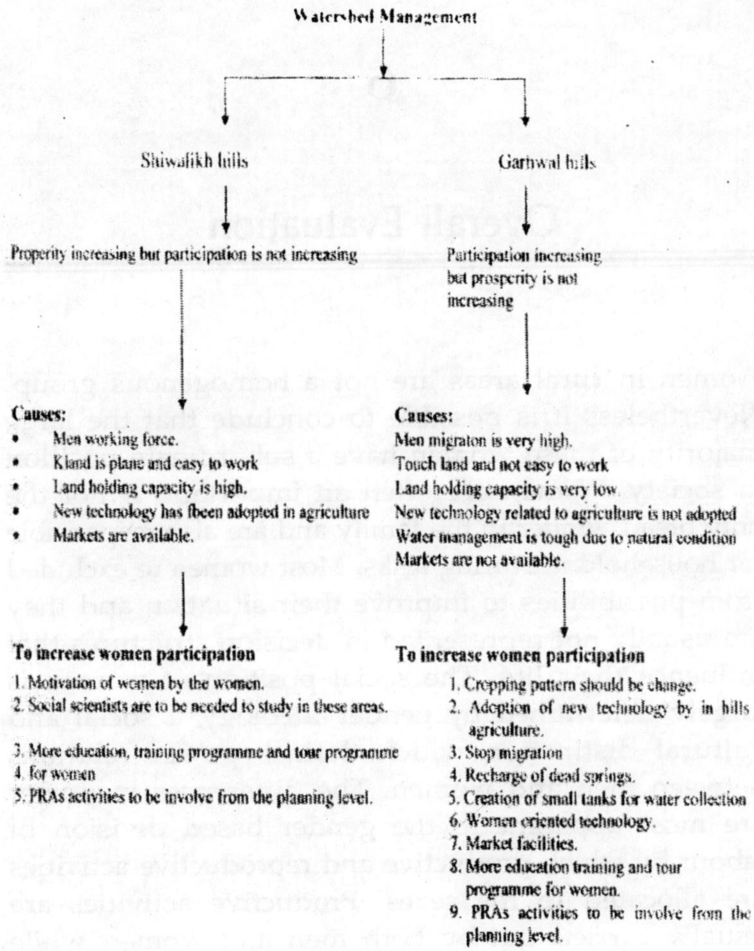
Watershed Management
Shiwalikh hills
Garhwal hills
Properity increasing but participation is not increasing
Participation increasing but prosperity is not increasing
Causes:
Men working force.
Kland is plane and easy to work
Land holding capacity is high.
New technology has fbeen adopted in agriculture
Markets are available.
Causes:
Men migraton is very high.
Touch land and not easy to work
Land holding capacity is very low.
New technology related to agriculture is not adopted
Water management is tough due to natural condition
Markets are not available.
To increase women participation
1. Motivation of women by the women.
2. Social scientists are to be needed to study in these areas.
3. More education, training programme and tour programme
4. for women
5. PRAs activities to be involve from the planning level.
To increase women participation
1. Cropping pattern should be change.
2. Adeption of new technology by in hills agriculture.
3. Stop migration
4. Recharge of dead springs.
5. Creation of small tanks for water collection
6. Women oriented technology.
7. Market facilities.
8. More education training and tour programme for women.
9. PRAs activities to be involve from the planning level.

6

Overall Evaluation

Women in rural areas are not a homogenous group. Nevertheless it is possible to conclude that the large majority of these women have a subordinate position in society. Women are often an important, if not the only bread winner in the family and are also responsible for household nurturing tasks. Most women re excluded from possibilities to improve their situation and they are usually not represented in decision structures that influence their life. The social position of women is largely determined by gender ideology, a social and cultural distinction which defines power relations between men and women. The differences in power are most apparent in the gender based division of labour by which productive and reproductive activities are allocated to the sexes. Productive activities are usually carried out by both men and women while only women are involved in reproductive activities. This results in what is commonly known as the double workload of women. In the process of carrying out productive and reproductive activities specific natural resources are tapped depending on the kind of activity.

Varying qualities and combinations of soil, water, air, vegetation and fauna are used as inputs. Due to task division between men and women there is also a differentiated use of natural resources between them. However women's ability to provide and sustain depended on their direct access to nature's resources and control over technology and their own labour, and the history of this early period is also the history of the systematic undermining of women's autonomy as agriculture producers in many parts of the globe.

Although rural women have contributed a lot in the growth of agriculture in India through various development programme yet these vary programmes have stimulated their marginalization. The reasons are manifold such as biological, cultural, mechanical, psychological/mythological and administrative. The relationship between women, men and environment is structured by gender differentiated roles, rights and responsibilities with respect to the use, management and ownership of natural resources. Without understanding this mechanism even environmental friendly efforts can result in increase pressure/ exploitation of farm women.

The overall environment decline in the country's natural resources base is manifested in deteriorating soil condition and depleting water and forest resources. According to official estimates about 200million ha representing almost 60 percent of the country's geographical area is affected by degradation problems of varying degrees. The effect of deforestation and disruption of the fragile ecological balance especially in the Himalayan region representing a quarter of India forest reserve is so great that this mighty mountain chain could become barren by the first half of the next century (Mahatet et al, 1986). The environmental degradation in the mountainous region also affects adversely the people living down below in the foothills.

The problems related to livelihood in the hilly ecosystems are somewhat different from those of plains. Two important features of foothill system are: (1) That most of the farmers have small and scattered land holding and in order to ameliorate their plight they keep large herds of cattle, which they are unable to feed from local natural and cultivated resources. As fodder scarcities increase, men are forced to migrate along with their cattle for 4 to 8 months in a year to areas there is enough supply in a fodder and water throughout the year. The role of women becomes much more pertinent as they significantly contribute to all land based operations including animal raring in addition to usual household chores. (2) When resources deplete due to soil erosion and denudation of hills, the rural women are particularly under stress as their livelihood is directly and strongly dependent upon natural resources. Depletion of land resources would mean increased struggle to produce the same or even less amount of food grain. Deforestation would mean more travel time to collect fuel and fodder. Diminishing water availability naturally means spending more time on fetching water from long distances.

Since it is women's activities that protect and conserve nature's bounty in forests and in agriculture in hilly ecosystems and through such conservation works she sustains human life through ensuring the availability of food, fodder and water, the destruction on the integrity of the forest ecosystem is most vividly and correctly experienced by peasant women. For them forest is the source of food production. It is essential for providing the fertility directly as green manure or as organic matter cycled through farm animals. Women agricultural work in regions like the Himalayas is largely work in and with the forest and other natural resources, yet it is discounted both in forestry and in agriculture.

Watershed management programmes which attempt to conserve natural resources tend to optimize farm and forest production and therefore were supposed to help in reducing drudgery of farm women to as great extent. The project focused on rainwater harvesting by constructing small earth dams and recycling of stored water through the system of underground pipelines to the adjoining farm lands through gravity. Land levelling and land shaping operations were also carried out on farm lands to efficiently utilize the limited water and to conserve rainwater in situ. Simultaneously, improved agronomic practices were introduced to maximum the return. There was two to four times increase in agricultural productivity as a result of supplemental irrigation. This is turn helped in linking the economic interests of the villagers to the protection of adjoining forests and preventing their further degradation. Due to the increased availability of fodder both from fields as well as forests, the dependence of villagers on forest also reduced. To encourage cooperation and participation of villagers for protecting forest areas and maintenance of dam and pipelines and distributing irrigation water, hill resource management societies were formed in the wsm village but women participation in these societies are very low in comparison to men. Women are aware about the activities but active participation of women is nil. The major problems of HRMS are: (1) the office bearers are not much interested in maintaining accounts and holding regular meetings. (2) Elections of the office bearers have not been held for some time. (3) cashiers are not trained to maintain the account of HRMS. (4) There is no audit system or any supervisory authorities are their. (5) The legal remedies in case of default are also not very clear. (6) The mode of expenditure or the items on which the society funds can be spent are not clearly stipulated. (7) many times village politics involved in such type of societies create problems in smooth working. Women are far behind from all the activities of HRMS.

Development has so far been restricted to economic issues only to the total disregard to the social and institutional framework of gender injustice and inequality. There are five important factors that had deprived women from natural resources they need: (1) resource depletion, (2) Changing family structure, (3) introduction of new technologies, (4) development of projects that fail to target women, and (5) Women's little access to crucial means of productions such as land, credit and associated production technology. In soil and water conservation programmes, solutions are sought for the problems called soil erosion. Such solutions are the result of a series of decision that are made of different levels and stages of a programme. All decisions include certain assumption based on the norms and values of planners. When these assumptions are in correct, not only the success of the land users both man and women, in the area of interaction. To understand the effects of a programme on women, it is necessary to examine the decision that are made during the course of a programme and the assumption on which they are based.

It is the time to help restore the precarious balance

between women and natural resources. While this can often be done by making simple changes in the development projects, it also requires high level policy support. It is increasingly obvious that the participation of women in natural resource management project is crucial for their success. Planners must consider women as well as men in their plans for development project.

In country like India it is the need of the time, as we are in process of developing, the development projects should taken the shape of movements. Small and experimental projects are not able to change the socioeconomic status of women. The most important things is that policy makers should two way to explore gender issues through recognising that the need of men and women may not be the same and that the impact of projects on them may therefore be different. Try to investigate the customs, taboos and time constrains that women face, realizing that knowledge and common sense can go long way to overcoming these constraints. They should also the promote the role that women do and can play in development activities at each level and analyze the ways in which projects either include or exclude them. It is important to exchange information with individuals at every level with women on forestry and soil conservation activities, with practitioners on involving women in projects, with policy makers on women's role in natural resources. They should also support women's groups and encourage the formation of new ones the help women gain access in decision making and the political process and strengthen women's support for one another. At the time of policy formation policy makers also work together to provide access to land and trees, thereby recognizing customary and traditional women holdings, ensuring women are included where land is privatized and seeking creative solutions for landless women. Collaboration for credit and income available to women either individually or through women's group are very important. It is always important to consult with women before introducing new technologies or species ensuring that woman's needs have been considered and the impact of new techniques on women's lives has been associated. And in the last there should be no gaps between policy makers and women of rural India. There gaps always deprived rural women from their share.

As per women problems are it is to be noticed that sensible policies can overcome some constraints. The first requirement is that women must be specifically targeted when projects are being formulated. The fundamental need is to evaluate a projects potential impact on and expected benefits to, both men and women separately. Gender issues need careful analysis unintended effects on either sex are to be avoided. Preliminary research may be needed to establish exactly how a project is likely to affect women. Such things are not always obvious. Enquiries need to be made into the needs, interests, talents and desire for participation of the women in communities to be affected by natural involving women in project design as well as project execution. Doing so can automatically eliminate some of the less desirable practices of the past. The role of women in the cash economy is another fundamental issue. Because women have traditionally operated in the subsistence sector, it is tempting to design projects to assist them only in their traditional roles. Women urgently need to be brought more fully into the cash economy, and to be provided with credit and security of land tenure on an equal basis with men. If gender issues are specifically identified early in project planning, further projects could break much new grounds. In the process both rural women and professionals gain a great deal. Enabling women to benefit fully from natural resources is likely to prove one of the most rewarding and environmentally benign ways of fighting rural poverty.

Another strategy for increasing women's voice could be to promote alliances between women of JFM groups and other local women in leadership positions. The elected women panchayat representatives fall in this category. Many villages nowhere women ward panches or sarpaches through whom women involved in JFM could develop better links with other panchayat activities. Alliances could also be built with aanganwari workers. Developments of Women and Children in Rural Area (DWCRA) groups and women organizers trained under state or central government programmes such as women's development programme in Rajasthan and mahila Samakhya in six states where these programme overlap with JFM areas. From the women point of view it is important to mention here that in the West Bengal forest development created a post for women co-ordinator in the principal chief conservator of forest (PCCF) office in 1994 and a women forest officer was also posted there. Her responsibilities are also: (1) Motivate women to become active Forest Protection Committee (FPC) members and orienting male members to support their participation, (2) motivating the departments field staff of promote women participation, and (3) promoting formation of women's sub-groups to ensure that the benefits accruing from income generating activities percolate to women members, and collecting in formation and data about women related activities from different divisions for dissemination to all concerned. Such type of post creation is also needed in other states and institutions like ICAR etc.

Women empowerment through participation has become a reality and need of the society. Women participation in development programme like watershed management has become central to Indian Policy making process as well as in society. Women full participation is essential to achieve the goal of women's empowerment. Women constitute half of the world's population, perform nearly two-third of its work hours, receive one-tenth of the world income and own less then one-hundredth of the world's property. Women constitute 48-09 percent of India's population. Her role is increasing day by day in each and every field of the society. In fact, women are establishing themserlf in every field which was previously represented by only male. In ninth plan draft, as it focus, "to create an enabling environment where women can truly exercise their rights and outside homes as equal partners along with men. The draft directs both the centre and the states to adopt the "women component Plan" through which no less than 30% of funds and benefits are earmarked to the women related sectors. There is no doubt that women's development is directly related to national development. The development of women's resources i.e., their abilities, interests, skills and other potentialities are of paramount importance fort the mobilization and development of human resources. In India it is right time for reviewing and amending laws and practices which discriminate against women and girl child and must be accompanied by a movement to bring about an attitudinal change in society.

The need of the hour is to equal women's participation in governance and the decision making process. A radical approach in women's perception of their empowerment role is of prime importance in the present times. Targets have to be fixed, carefully based on micro and macro level planning and a regular monitoring system can lead to definite achievements. To enable women to fight against any hurdles, it is necessary to empower them by ensuring their participation in decision making bodies at all levels. With the emergence of gender as one of the key issues of human progress, women who have been identified as a disempowered and therefore a 'non-productive' sector need to be brought into the mainstream of development.

Why women's participation is so important for their empowerment and development. The answer is very simple and straight. There can be no real power in democratic world without the equal participation of women and men in all spheres of life and different levels of decision making. The goals of development with human face cannot be attained without women's full participation not only in the development process, but also in shaping its goals targets. Women's participation is changing the world in which we live by bringing new priorities and perspectives to the political process and the organisation of society. In focusing attention on the most neglected and most deprived section of humanity today, women and girls, women's participation will make society more responsive to the needs of all people. Women's participation in socio-economic and political process will bring quantitative and qualitative change in the life of most vulnerable section of the society and bring them into the mainstream. In Jack Lang's words if "Tomorrow belongs to women", the groundwork for it must begin from today itself on war footing.

It emerged from this study that:

(1) Women have contributed in rural development although they are poor, unlettered and inexperienced. (2) Where women associated with Mahila Mandal or any social organisation perform better than those who have not associated such organizations. (3) Their assetlessness, illiteracy and ignorance are the three basic. Problems which constrain them to perform their role as members and mangers of the natural resources and managers of the natural resources. (4) Land plays an important role in the power structure in rural India. The ground reality is without land ownership, they are not safe even their own households. It is surprising to note that the agricultural census does not have the classification of women vis-à-vis others. (5) It is well known that about 33 percent of the rural population live below the poverty line, according to the 43rd round of National Sample Survey Organisation. A majority of them are women. If land and assets are transferred in their favour, they sustain their livelihood properly and organise themselves to participate in village or block or Zilla affairs through women organisations. (6) It may be mentioned here that about 30 percent of the rural households have been headed by women who bear all the burden for the families. There are certain legislators such as Zamindari Abolition Act which go against economic empowerment of women. Such type of legislation may be made women. Friendly for their betterment.

After more than five decades of planning in India women are for below their counterparts. The main reason for such plight of women has been their non-involvement and participation in decision in governance and development.

Despite the accumulation forces for a greater participation for over all development, large member of people continued to be excluded from the benefits of development especially the weaker section of society including women.

Women have distinct role to play in the development of the nation. In the role of a mother, women shapes the personality and character of her children and hence the character of the nation. As a house wife, she maintains the productivity of human capital within the household through proper management of home. Apart from this, a women herself represents a unity of human capital, and is therefore capable of making contribution to the economy of the nation. For a country like ours, people both male and female are the only abundant asset. Women constitute nearly half of the population. There can not be true development or growth of a nation with half its population living in ignorance, withdraw from the mainstream unrecognized, and unaccounted for. In this background, women rank as very important resource in the national development.

The UN development report puts it "Development must be participatory and for this, people must have the opportunity to participate and to invest in the development of their capacities. All the citizens must have the opportunity to put their capabilities to use, to be fully involved in all aspects of life, to express themselves freely and collectively. In India the 73rd and 74th amendment acts have provided such an opportunity for women. Factors affecting of development are many and they effects the decision making ability of women. Factors affecting women's ability to participate in the process of development are many and they effects the decision making certain image has been given to them that is a household status. (2) Poor educational and training background (3) Poor health status. Effective participation of all women in development as intellectual, policy makers and decision-makers, planners, contributors and beneficiaries should be strengthened according to specific problems of women in different regions and the needs of different categories of women in them. That commitment on the part of policy makers should guide the formulation and implementation of policies, Plans, programmes and projects will be improved and society advanced through the full and effective participation of women.

In most parts of the country, and particularly among marginal and landless agriculturists, earning a livelihood is still a family endeavour. Various studies conducted and this study also have clearly pointed out that there are a large number of women who primarily derive their livelihood from working, sometimes on a regular basis and often on a seasonal basis, or attached labours. These women generally belong to illiterate SC, ST and backward classes. In Relmajra near all about 200 families are land less and all is SC, working as a labour to the fields of others.

The major agricultural operations in which women generally work are transplanting, harvesting, cutting twigs clearing the fields. They collect cowdung for fuel and manure. They cut grass and sell it as fodder. They travel long distances and cut or collect firewood and sell it or bring it home for use. They do these and many other income brining bobs in addiction to the household chores. Women belonging to tenant and small land owning families also work on their own lands, both actively and in supervisory roles. They also have technical knowledge of cultivation and hire labourers and supervise their work. In spite of doing all these work many of these women are very often listed in the census under the category of 'non-workers'. Their work is not always counted and recorded. Gail Omvedt has emphasized that woman's tasks though very crucial and involving skills which have been acquired over generations are treated as less important and of lower worth. Gail Omvedt also questions the assumption that women cannot be trained for the higher jobs, which pay more. Modernisation and development thus further marginalizes women and leads to large scale displacements of women from agricultural employment. According to this study it is very clear that women are paid less than men, they contribute a higher proportion of their earning to the household than the man. The women also feel that their main responsibility is the care of their children. Among the agriculture labourers especially the Harijan women's work is still valued and women's position remains higher among the tenants and middle peasants.

Thus, if land reforms are properly implemented conditions of women, giving them increased economic independence and an opportunity to march towards greater equality in legal, social and political rights.

The crux of the matter is the subordinate status accorded to women by the male dominated society. This must be attacked internally at its cultural roots and externally by deliberately promoting women in status and position in society. Greater participation of women in social and political life is equally important for their integration of them in the development in a man made "Women development programme" women are made leader of Mahila Mandali. While man leads the society, woman made leader of women group. Politics is a decision making organisation. In village to national politics decides future of the society and nation. Women is equally a part of society. Therefore for a meaningful development, women must have say in politics. Therefore she must become a leader of the society like man and not women group only. The development policy that we have today is largely exploitative of nature and women. To achieve some kind stable change, it is important that we alter the whole concept of development with emphasis on women's role and participation from planning to monitoring. Caught between poverty and environmental destruction poor rural women in villages could well be reaching an endurance limit. The status of women makes it difficult. For them to go organized or to get them organised. Women must be integrated into the process of rural development not only because simple justice demands that it to be done, but also because excluding women means under utilization of high potential resource that will adversely affect the economic growth rate.

Women are repositories of the vast knowledge of indigenous farming methods, seeds, crop-rotation, and terracing and water conservation. There is a need to develop channels at the project time to absorb this indigenous native wisdom of women to supplement most of the mega politics of development in villages.

Women groups should be consulted prior to a deal over their usable item. In the present era women have to play a very active role in controlling her resources from unfair trade pacts.

As size of landholding decrease, villagers need to become more and more dependent on so called appropriate technology. This new technology is referred to as a 'women friendly technology' since it emerges out of the needs of women like solar-cooker, biogas plants, power from water, improved bullock carts and alternative housing design are techniques which do not extract out of women's reserves in the village but on the contrary contribute to their upkeep.

Annexure I

Format used for collection of information before and after project
Diagnostic survey on women's in WSM details of respondent

1. Name of the Block : ____________ Name of respondent : ____________
2. Name of the Gramsabha : ____________ Name of head of the family: ____________
3. Name of the village : ____________ Name of watershed: ____________
Priod ____________

Family description:

Name	Age	Education	Occupation	Remarks

WOMEN AND PLANNING OF WSM

Activities	Women response to activities	What are the major constraints in participation in planning	How they can participate in planning more and more	Remarks
1. Talking to village women at the time of planning of WSM	A. Occasionally B. Frequently C. Never			
2. Conducting meetings of women at the time of planning	D. Many times E. Thrice pearl planning F. Twice pearl planning G. Once H. Never			
3. Training of women for WSM	I. One training programme J. Two training programme			
4. film show for women	One show Two show			
5. Pre-survey of WSM and women consent	They have some idea No idea of survey They do not know about survey			
6. Other				

WOMEN AND LAND HOLDING

Land related information	Size of land Nali/ha		Differentiation in land		Suggestion for land	Remarks
	Before project	After project	Increasing factors	Decreasing factors		
A. Owned land						
B. Irrigated land						
C. Unirrigated land						
D. Kharif irrigated						
E. Zaid irrigated						
F. Land less						

Time allocation by farmer women in a day

Activities	Time spend on activity		Differentiation in time in month
	Before Project	After Project	J.................................D
1. Houschold/including child care			J.................................D
2. Agriculture/crop			J.................................D
3. livestock/cleaning and milking			J.................................D
4. Fodder collection			J.................................D
5. Fuel collection			J.................................D
6. Fetching water			J.................................D
7. Entertainment			J.................................D
8. Social activities			J.................................D
9. Other if any			J.................................D
10. Rest			J.................................D

WOMEN AND AGRICULTURE

Activities	Time spend on activities		Reason behind time differentiation		Suggestion for in which activities time should increase and decrease and how?	Remarks
	Before project	After project	Time increasing factors	Time decreasing factors		
A. Cultivation						
B. Ploughing						
C. Transplantation						
D. Fertilizer						
E. Irrigation						
F. Weeding						
G. Threshing						
H. Cleaning						
I. Storage						
J. Preparation for marketing						
K. Other						

WOMEN AND HORTICULTURE

Activities	Time spend on activities		Reason behind time differentiation		Suggestion for in which activities time should increase and decrease and how?	Remarks
	Before project	After project	Time increasing factors	Time decreasing factors		
A. Land selection						
B. Land preparation						
C. Plantation						
D. Watering						
E. Use of fertilizers						
F. Use of insecticide and pesticide						
G. Collection of fruits						
H. Storage						
I. Preparation for marketing						
J. Other						

WOMEN AND CASH CROP

Activities	Time spend on activities		Reason behind time differentiation		Suggestion for in which activities time should increase and decrease and how?	Remarks
	Before project	After project	Time increasing factors	Time decreasing factors		
A. Land preparation						
B. Plantation						
C. Watering						
D. Use of fertilizers						
E. Use of insecticide and pesticide						
F. Collection of cash crop						
G. Storage						
H. Preparation for market						
I. Other						

WOMEN AND LIVESTOCK

Activities	Time spend on activities		Reason behind time differentiation		Suggestion for in which activities time should increase and decrease and how?	Remarks
	Before project	After project	Time increasing factors	Time decreasing factors		
A. Grazing						
B. Chaffing of fodder						
C. Cleaning the animals and cattlesheds						
D. Milking						
E. Preparation of dung cake						
F. Processing of milk						
G. Other						

WOMEN AND FODDER COLLECTION

Factors	**Fodder consumption**		**Differentiation in consumption**		**Suggestion for different factors**	**Remarks**
	Before Project	After Project	Consumption increasing factors	Consumption decreasing factors		
A. Amount of fodder consumption per day per family						
		Differentiation in frequency to go to collecting the fodder				
B. Frequency to go to collecting the fodder from forest	Every day J-------------D Once a week J-------------D Twice a week J-------------D Once a month J-------------D		Frequency increasing Factors - - -	Frequency Decreasing Factors		
		Differentiation in distances				
C. Distances traveled for collecting fodder from forest	Less than 2km J-------------D 2 to 4 km J-------------D 4 to 6 km J-------------D >6 km J-------------D		Distance increasing factors	Distances decreasing factors		

WOMEN AND FUEL COLLECTION

Factors	Fuel consumption		Differentiation in consumption		Suggestion for different factors	Remarks
	Before Project	After Project	Increasing factors	Decreasing factors		
A. Amount of fuel consumption per day per family	.					
		Differentiation in frequency to go to forest for fodder				
B. Frequency to go to collecting the fuel from forest	Every day J- -------------D Once a week J- ------------D Twice a week J- -------------D Once a month J- -------------D		Difference increasing Factors - - -	Difference Decreasing Factors		
			Differentiation in distance			
C. Distances traveled for collecting fuel wood	Every day J- -----------D Once a week J- -- ---------D Twice a week J- ------------D Once a month J- ------------D		Distance increasing factors -	Distances decreasing factors		

WOMEN AND ECONOMIC ACTIVITIES

Factors	Income in a year		Differentiation in consumption		Suggestion for increasing the income from different factors and how?	Remarks
	Before Project	After Project	Increasing factors	Decreasin g factors		
A. Farming						
B. Daring						
C. Sale of animal						
D. Wage income						
E. Trading						
F. Hiring						
G. Service						
H. Horticulture						
I. Other						

Annexure II

Questionnaire Used for Survey

Q.1 When the project was started?

Q.2 Do you have any idea about the project before it was implemented in your village? (Yes/No)

Q.3 If yes, how you came to know about the project.

Q.4 Is there any meeting of the villagers was held with the officials of implementing agency. (Yes/No)

Q.5 How many meetings were held/

Q.6 Who participated in these meetings?

Q.7 What was the major agenda of that meeting?

Q.8 Have you participated in these meetings?

Q.9 If yes, was your voice was noticed by officials 100%, 50% 25%, 0%.

Q.10 If no, then what are the reasons? It is possible for you to mention one or two?

Q.11 What are the possible methods/ways to overcome from these reasons?

Q.12 Do you have any knowledge about the survey which was conducted in the village for watershed management? (Yes/No)

Q.13 If yes, have you been interviewed (Yes/No)

Q.14 If no, then who have been interviewed – only village elite/leaders/persons accessible to them on an average all persons family representatives.

Q.15 Do they discuss the project plan with villagers? (Yes/No)

Q.16 If yes, whether the plan was as per your requirement? (Yes/No)

Q.17 If no, what are the modifications were needed from your point of view?

Q.18 Are they taken care of by project officials?

Q.19 If yes, what were the major suggestions from your side?

Q.20 If no, what are the problems you are facing just because of your suggestion was not implemented?

Q.21 Do you have any idea in your mind to modification the present going on project?

Q.22 If yes, what is the idea and have you taken any initiatives for that.

Q.23 If yes, what are the initiatives you have taken?

Implementation

Q.24 When the project activities were actually implemented in your fields.

Q.25 What are these activities?

Q.26 Whether you are informed about the time of starting the activity?

Q.27 If yes, is it helped in management of other activities?

Q.28 Have you participated in these activities (Yes/No)

Q.29 If yes, how

Name of the Activity

Name of the activity	*Level of participation*	
	Family	Women

What you have achieved

Technical Financial Other

Q.30 How you evaluate your participation

A good experience

No experience

Q.31 If good, is it continue till today and if not continue what are the major constraints.

Q.32 How we can overcome through these constraints?

Q.33 Do the project officials record some data during the project? (Yes/No)

Q.34 If yes, then what type of data they were collecting?

Q.35 Have you taken part in any of such activities in which manner?

Q.36 Did you find any difference between your

traditional and demonstrated technology? (Yes/No)

Q.37 If yes, then what and which extent (with activities)

The name of activities

Q.38 How you measure it.

Q.39 Are you adopting all these activities? (Yes/No)

Q.40 What are the reasons for adopting/rejecting the new technologies?

Q.41 What were your expectations from the project?

Q.42 Did you achieved them or not?

Q.43 What are your personal gains from the project?

Q.44 Please tell us about the specific gains?

Q.45 What are you planning to continue these gains?

Q.46 If yes, do you tell us about the major profits?

Q.47 If no, what are the major problems?

Q.48 How we can solve the above obstacles to your point of view.

Q.49 Do you want to say anything new in a detailed manner about the water management in your village.

Annexure III

Sl. No.	Name	Age	Education	Village	Watershed
1	Sona	26	7th Pass	Sukhomajri	Sukhomajri
2	Binro	70	Illiterate	Sukhomajri	Sukhomajri
3	Satya Devi	30	Illiterate	Sukhomajri	Sukhomajri
4	Mohini Devi	15	10th Pass	Sukhomajri	Sukhomajri
5	Saroj	35	Illiterate	Sukhomajri	Sukhomajri
6	Pansini Devi	70	Illiterate	Sukhomajri	Sukhomajri
7	Poorni Devi	40	Illiterate	Sukhomajri	Sukhomajri
8	Mindro	35	Illiterate	Sukhomajri	Sukhomajri
9	Ramasri	33	Illiterate	Sukhomajri	Sukhomajri
10	Dayalo	30	Illiterate	Sukhomajri	Sukhomajri
11	Usha	32	10th pass	Sukhomajri	Sukhomajri
12	Manti	40	Illiterate	Sukhomajri	Sukhomajri
13	Moni	18	M.A.	Sukhomajri	Sukhomajri
14	Sulochana Devi	25	Illiterate	Sukhomajri	Sukhomajri
15	Santo Devi	70	Illiterate	Sukhomajri	Sukhomajri
16	Chinto Devi	60	Illiterate	Sukhomajri	Sukhomajri
17	Salinder	28	Illiterate	Sukhomajri	Sukhomajri
18	Kamla	23	Illiterate	Sukhomajri	Sukhomajri
19	Kapooro	60	Illiterate	Sukhomajri	Sukhomajri
20	Pago	28	Illiterate	Sukhomajri	Sukhomajri
21	Ganga Devi	38	Illiterate	Sukhomajri	Sukhomajri
22	Parveen	18	8th Pass	Sukhomajri	Sukhomajri
23	Krishna Devi	30	Illiterate	Sukhomajri	Sukhomajri
24	Sikha Devi	26	Illiterate	Sukhomajri	Sukhomajri

25	Sito Devi	50	Illiterate	Sukhomajri	Sukhomajri
26	Chaya	24	Illiterate	Sukhomajri	Sukhomajri
27	Saroj	28	6th Pass	Sukhomajri	Sukhomajri
28	Karni Devi	70	Illiterate	Sukhomajri	Sukhomajri
29	Bachani Devi	40	Illiterate	Sukhomajri	Sukhomajri
30	Rekha	18	5th pass	Sukhomajri	Sukhomajri
31	Vidya Devi	36	Illiterate	Sukhomajri	Sukhomajri
32	Paramjeet Kaur	20	8th pass	Sukhomajri	Sukhomajri
33	Krishna	37	6th pass	Sukhomajri	Sukhomajri
34	Sumati	24	Illiterate	Sukhomajri	Sukhomajri
35	Pyari Devi	40	5th pass	Sukhomajri	Sukhomajri
36	Savvitri Devi	42	5th pass	Sukhomajri	Sukhomajri
37	Tejo	20	5th pass	Sukhomajri	Sukhomajri
38	Krishna	40	Illiterate	Sukhomajri	Sukhomajri
39	Sushma	17	10th pass	Sukhomajri	Sukhomajri
40	Soma Devi	50	Illiterate	Sukhomajri	Sukhomajri
41	Mena	20	8th pass	Sukhomajri	Sukhomajri
42	Jito	40	Illiterate	Sukhomajri	Sukhomajri
43	Pago	70	Illiterate	Sukhomajri	Sukhomajri
44	Raj Kumari	20	Illiterate	Sukhomajri	Sukhomajri
45	Laxmi	25	Illiterate	Sukhomajri	Sukhomajri
46	Maya	30	Illiterate	Sukhomajri	Sukhomajri
47	Karmi	70	Illiterate	Sukhomajri	Sukhomajri
48	Pyari Devi	25	Illiterate	Sukhomajri	Sukhomajri
49	Socha Devi	40	Illiterate	Sukhomajri	Sukhomajri
50	Defo	35	Illiterate	Sukhomajri	Sukhomajri
51	Pago Devi	40	Illiterate	Sukhomajri	Sukhomajri
52	Vidya Devi	40	Illiterate	Sukhomajri	Sukhomajri
53	Kawaro	70	Illiterate	Sukhomajri	Sukhomajri
54	Kamla Devi	30	Illiterate	Sukhomajri	Sukhomajri
55	Pyari	60	Illiterate	Sukhomajri	Sukhomajri
56	Prito	40	Illiterate	Sukhomajri	Sukhomajri
57	Bachani Devi	45	Illiterate	Sukhomajri	Sukhomajri
58	Haldeep	28	8th pass	Sukhomajri	Sukhomajri
59	Parseen	70.	Illiterate	Sukhomajri	Sukhomajri
60	Rosni	35	Illiterate	Sukhomajri	Sukhomajri
61	Sulochana Devi	42	5th pass	Sukhomajri	Sukhomajri
62	Nimo	80	Illiterate	Sukhomajri	Sukhomajri
63	Vimla Devi	36	5th pass	Sukhomajri	Sukhomajri
64	Premi Devi	65	Illiterate	Sukhomajri	Sukhomajri

Respondent of Relmajra Watershed Management

Sl. No.	*Name*	*Age*	*Education*	*Village*	*Watershed*
1	Kiran Balan	30	12th pass	Relmajra	Relmajra
2	Raj Rani	60	Illiterate	Relmajra	Relmajra
3	Laxmi Devi	25	5th pass	Relmajra	Relmajra
4	Kiran negi	22	8th pass	Relmajra	Relmajra
5	Mito Devi	35	Illiterate	Relmajra	Relmajra
6	Satya Devi	45	Illiterate	Relmajra	Relmajra
7	Babli	20	5th pass	Relmajra	Relmajra
8	Karna Devi	28	Illiterate	Relmajra	Relmajra
9	Geeta	30	Illiterate	Relmajra	Relmajra
10	Manso Devi	60	Illiterate	Relmajra	Relmajra
11	Darshan Kaur	20	10th pass	Relmajra	Relmajra
12	Gurmito	40	Illiterate	Relmajra	Relmajra
13	Manjeet Kaur	16	8th pass	Relmajra	Relmajra
14	Mamta Rani	15	Studying in 10th	Relmajra	Relmajra
15	Mito Devi	30	Illiterate	Relmajra	Relmajra
16	Amro Devi	60	Illiterate	Relmajra	Relmajra
17	Darshan Devi	18	7th pass	Relmajra	Relmajra
18	Amro Devi II	55	Illiterate	Relmajra	Relmajra
19	Poli	25	8th pass	Relmajra	Relmajra
20	Mindo Devi	35	Illiterate	Relmajra	Relmajra
21	Laxmi Devi	50	Illiterate	Relmajra	Relmajra
22	Bimla Devi	45	5th pass	Relmajra	Relmajra
23	Seema Devi	15	8th pas	Relmajra	Relmajra
24	Bachani Devi	50	Illiterate	Relmajra	Relmajra
25	Ninder Devi	25	Illiterate	Relmajra	Relmajra
26	Parveen	24	10th pass	Relmajra	Relmajra
27	Poli Devi	20	Illiterate	Relmajra	Relmajra
28	Shakuntla	21	5th pass	Relmajra	Relmajra
29	Jitoo Devi	45	Illiterate	Relmajra	Relmajra
30	Manjeet	18	10th pass	Relmajra	Relmajra
31	Jeto	40	Illiterate	Relmajra	Relmajra
32	Kanta	20	10th pass	Relmajra	Relmajra
33	Pushpa	22	8th pass	Relmajra	Relmajra
34	Manander Kaur	15	8th going	Relmajra	Relmajra
35	Santosh	14	5th pass	Relmajra	Relmajra
36	Amro Devi	60	Illiterate	Relmajra	Relmajra
37	Bimla Devi	35	5th pass	Relmajra	Relmajra
38	Krishna Devi	30	IInd pass	Relmajra	Relmajra
39	Geeta Devi	40	Illiterate	Relmajra	Relmajra
40	Premlata	19	10th pass	Relmajra	Relmajra
41	Kala Rani	60	Illiterate	Relmajra	Relmajra
42	Sasi Bala	35	Illiterate	Relmajra	Relmajra

43	Rani Devi	25	10th pass	Relmajra	Relmajra
44	Krishna	35	Illiterate	Relmajra	Relmajra
45	Bachan	45	Illiterate (Widow)	Relmajra	Relmajra
46	Manju	21	10th (Widow)	Relmajra	Relmajra
47	Bimla Devi	27	5th pass	Relmajra	Relmajra
48	Daya	90	Illiterate	Relmajra	Relmajra
49	Shanti	80	Illiterate	Relmajra	Relmajra
50	Usha	23	10th pass	Relmajra	Relmajra
51	Geeta Devi	45	Illiterate	Relmajra	Relmajra
52	Mindo Devi	30	Illiterate	Relmajra	Relmajra
53	Dhanti Devi	70	Illiterate	Relmajra	Relmajra
54	Bachani Devi	35	Illiterate	Relmajra	Relmajra
55	Babi	18	10th pass	Relmajra	Relmajra
56	Kanta	16	10th pass	Relmajra	Relmajra
57	Santi	82	Illiterate	Relmajra	Relmajra
58	Harbhajan Kaur	40	3rd pass	Relmajra	Relmajra
59	Kirna	16	7th pass	Relmajra	Relmajra
60	Gurmit Kaur	46	5th pass	Relmajra	Relmajra
61	Suman Deep	20	10th pass	Relmajra	Relmajra
62	Kanta Devi	17	6th pass	Relmajra	Relmajra
63	Meto	60	Illiterate	Relmajra	Relmajra

Respondent of Harijan Women or Landless Women Relmajra Watershed Management

Sl. No.	*Name*	*Age*	*Education*	*Village*	*Watershed*
1	Dharma Kaur	60	Illiterate	Relmajra	Relmajra
2	Satya Devi	35	Illiterate	Relmajra	Relmajra
3	Panjano	45	Illiterate	Relmajra	Relmajra
4	Rita	30	Illiterate	Relmajra	Relmajra
5	Manjeet	25	Illiterate	Relmajra	Relmajra
6	Sukh Devi	30	8th pass	Relmajra	Relmajra
7	Satya Devi II	40	Illiterate	Relmajra	Relmajra
8	Pyari Devi	45	Illiterate	Relmajra	Relmajra
9	Manjeet Kaur	25	Illiterate	Relmajra	Relmajra
10	Rajvinder	23	8th pass	Relmajra	Relmajra
11	Paramjeet	20	Illiterate	Relmajra	Relmajra
12	Kamla	35	Illiterate	Relmajra	Relmajra
13	Amro	60	Illiterate	Relmajra	Relmajra
14	Kamla	30	Illiterate	Relmajra	Relmajra
15	Rasmo	30	Illiterate	Relmajra	Relmajra
16	Paramjeet	22	5th pass	Relmajra	Relmajra
17	Debo	45	5th pass	Relmajra	Relmajra
18	Priti	14	5th pass	Relmajra	Relmajra
19	Baladev Kaur	45	Illiterate	Relmajra	Relmajra

Respondent of Bhuvneshwari Mahila Ashram Watershed Management

Sl. No.	*Name*	*Age*	*Education*	*Village*	*Watershed*
1	Usha Devi	45	Illiterate	Santoli	(Chandra Badni and Danda Watershed of BMA, NGO)
2	Urmila Devi	30	9th pass	Santoli	(Chandra Badni and Danda Watershed of BMA, NGO)
3	Bhagwani	50	Illiterate	Santoli	(Chandra Badni and Danda Watershed of BMA, NGO)
4	Mangli Devi	55	Illiterate	Santoli	(Chandra Badni and Danda Watershed of BMA, NGO)
5	Sarojni	33	Illiterate	Santoli	(Chandra Badni and Danda Watershed of BMA, NGO)
6	Basanti	40	Illiterate	Rupali	(Chandra Badni and Danda Watershed of BMA, NGO)
7	Kamla	40	Illiterate	Rupali	(Chandra Badni and Danda Watershed of BMA, NGO)
8	Bimla	40	5th pass	Santoli	(Chandra Badni and Danda Watershed of BMA, NGO)
9	Rajeshwari	35	Illiterate	Santoli	(Chandra Badni and Danda Watershed of BMA, NGO)
10	Darshani	28	Illiterate	Linghat	(Chandra Badni and Danda

					Watershed of BMA, NGO)
11	Nima	22	12th pass	Linghat	(Chandra Badni and Danda Watershed of BMA, NGO)
12	Sabha	75	Illiterate	Linghat	(Chandra Badni and Danda Watershed of BMA, NGO)
13	Sobha Devi	33	Illiterate	Linghat	(Chandra Badni and Danda Watershed of BMA, NGO)
14	Rajni	45	Illiterate	Linghat	(Chandra Badni and Danda Watershed of BMA, NGO)
15	Darshani Devi	62	Illiterate	Santoli	(Chandra Badni and Danda Watershed of BMA, NGO)
16	Cheta Devi	92	Illiterate	Santoli	(Chandra Badni and Danda Watershed of BMA, NGO)
17	Usha Devi	40	Illiterate	Santoli	(Chandra Badni and Danda Watershed of BMA, NGO)
18	Raksha Devi	24	Illiterate	Santoli	(Chandra Badni and Danda Watershed of BMA, NGO)
19	Chandra Devi	50	Illiterate	Kandiali	(Chandra Badni and Danda Watershed of BMA, NGO)
20	Urmila	21	Illiterate	Kandiali	(Chandra Badni and Danda Watershed of BMA, NGO)
21	Laxmi	50	8th pass	Kandiali	(Chandra Badni

				and Danda Watershed of BMA, NGO)
22 Parvati	75	Illiterate	Kandiali	(Chandra Badni and Danda Watershed of BMA, NGO)
23 Sampati	55	Illiterate	Kandiali	(Chandra Badni and Danda Watershed of BMA, NGO)
24 Rekha	21	12th pass	Kandiali	(Chandra Badni and Danda Watershed of BMA, NGO)
25 Permeshwari	19	12th pass	Kandiali	(Chandra Badni and Danda Watershed of BMA, NGO)
26 Makani Devi	40	Illiterate	Jhald.	(Chandra Badni and Danda Watershed of BMA, NGO)
27 Urmila	24	8th pass	Jhald.	(Chandra Badni and Danda Watershed of BMA, NGO)
28 Surma Devi	50	Illiterate	Jhald.	(Chandra Badni and Danda Watershed of BMA, NGO)
29 Mamta	17	10th pass	Jhald.	(Chandra Badni and Danda Watershed of BMA, NGO)
30 Naraini Devi	40	Illiterate	Jhald.	(Chandra Badni and Danda Watershed of BMA, NGO)
31 Besaki Devi	45	Illiterate	Jhald.	(Chandra Badni and Danda Watershed of BMA, NGO)

32	Satyeshwari	60	Illiterate	Jhald.	(Chandra Badni and Danda Watershed of BMA, NGO)
33	Babli	14	5th pass	Jhald.	(Chandra Badni and Danda Watershed of BMA, NGO)
34	Rani	45	Ist pass	Jhald.	(Chandra Badni and Danda Watershed of BMA, NGO)
35	Bimla Devi	35	Illiterate	Jhald.	(Chandra Badni and Danda Watershed of BMA, NGO)
36	Sumati	45	Illiterate	Jhald.	(Chandra Badni and Danda Watershed of BMA, NGO)
37	Sangeeta	18	10th pass	Jhald.	(Chandra Badni and Danda Watershed of BMA, NGO)
38	Ram Chandri	70	Illiterate	Jhald.	(Chandra Badni and Danda Watershed of BMA, NGO)
39	Laxmi	40	Illiterate	Pawala	(Chandra Badni and Danda Watershed of BMA, NGO)
40	Babli	17	10th going	Pawala	(Chandra Badni and Danda Watershed of BMA, NGO)
41	Gyani Devi	50	Illiterate	Pawala	(Chandra Badni and Danda Watershed of BMA, NGO)
42	Sajni	17	Illiterate	Pawala	(Chandra Badni and Danda Watershed of BMA, NGO)

43	Pushpa Devi	30	Illiterate	Pawala	(Chandra Badni and Danda Watershed of BMA, NGO)
44	Shakuntala Devi	45	Illiterate	Pawala	(Chandra Badni and Danda Watershed of BMA, NGO)
45	Bhuma Devi	30	8th pass	Pawala	(Chandra Badni and Danda Watershed of BMA, NGO)
46	Kamla Devi	36	Illiterate	Pawala	(Chandra Badni and Danda Watershed of BMA, NGO)
47	Chanki Devi	37	Illiterate	Pawala	(Chandra Badni and Danda Watershed of BMA, NGO)
48	Champa Devi	50	Illiterate	Pawala	(Chandra Badni and Danda Watershed of BMA, NGO)
49	Naraindevi	40	2nd pass	Pawala	(Chandra Badni and Danda Watershed of BMA, NGO)
50	Duga Devi	40	Illiterate	Pawala	(Chandra Badni and Danda Watershed of BMA, NGO)
51	Radha devi	25	5th pass	Pawala	(Chandra Badni and Danda Watershed of BMA, NGO)
52	Shakuntala Devi	40	Illiterate	Toli	(Chandra Badni and Danda Watershed of BMA, NGO)
53	Sangeeta	20	10th pass	Toli	(Chandra Badni and Danda Watershed of BMA, NGO)

54	Pyari Devi	40	Illiterate	Toli	(Chandra Badni and Danda Watershed of BMA, NGO)
55	Laxmi	28	Illiterate	Toli	(Chandra Badni and Danda Watershed of BMA, NGO)
56	Laxmi	50	Illiterate	Toli	(Chandra Badni and Danda Watershed of BMA, NGO)
57	Sangeeta	19	5th pass	Toli	(Chandra Badni and Danda Watershed of BMA, NGO)
58	Sarda Devi	24	8th pass	Toli	(Chandra Badni and Danda Watershed of BMA, NGO)
59	Poonam Devi	55	Illiterate	Toli	(Chandra Badni and Danda Watershed of BMA, NGO)
60	Sabti Devi	70	Illiterate	Toli	(Chandra Badni and Danda Watershed of BMA, NGO)
61	Sundri Devi	30	Illiterate	Toli	(Chandra Badni and Danda Watershed of BMA, NGO)
62	Gudi	45	Illiterate	Toli	(Chandra Badni and Danda Watershed of BMA, NGO)
63	Parvati	65	Illiterate	Toli	(Chandra Badni and Danda Watershed of BMA, NGO)
64	Rupa Devi	36	Illiterate	Toli	(Chandra Badni and Danda Watershed of BMA, NGO)

65	Sangeeta	18	10th going	Toli	(Chandra Badni and Danda Watershed of BMA, NGO)
66	Dupa	70	Illiterate	Toli	(Chandra Badni and Danda Watershed of BMA, NGO)
67	Deepa Devi	40	Illiterate	Toli	(Chandra Badni and Danda Watershed of BMA, NGO)
68	Ghapa devi	68	Illiterate	Toli	(Chandra Badni and Danda Watershed of BMA, NGO)
69	Laxmi	35	Illiterate	Toli	(Chandra Badni and Danda Watershed of BMA, NGO)

Respondent Chandrabhaga Watershed

Sl. No.	*Name*	*Age*	*Education*	*Village*	*Watershed*
1	Rejeshwari	36	3rd pass	Talai	Chandrabhaga
2	Ekta	26	12th pass	Talai	Chandrabhaga
3	Seema	18	9th pass	Talai	Chandrabhaga
4	Sheela Devi	49	8th pass	Talai	Chandrabhaga
5	Reena	22	B.A.	Talai	Chandrabhaga
6	Neeta	19	B.A.	Talai	Chandrabhaga
7	Dhani Devi	40	3rd pass	Talai	Chandrabhaga
8	Anita	22	10th pass	Talai	Chandrabhaga
9	Ravita	20	10th pass	Talai	Chandrabhaga
10	Meera Devi	40	Illiterate	Talai	Chandrabhaga
11	Magni Devi	43	1st pass	Talai	Chandrabhaga
12	Roshni	20	12th pass	Talai	Chandrabhaga
13	Darshani Devi	65	Illiterate	Talai	Chandrabhaga
14	Krishna	40	Illiterate	Talai	Chandrabhaga
15	Basanti	40	Illiterate	Talai	Chandrabhaga
16	Basanti	32	2nd pass	Talai	Chandrabhaga

17	Deepa	28	3rd pass	Talai	Chandrabhaga
18	Kamla	23	5th pass	Talai	Chandrabhaga
19	Guddi	20	5th pass	Talai	Chandrabhaga
20	Ujala Devi	50	Illiterate pass	Talai	Chandrabhaga
21	Nishi Devi	25	M.A.	Talai	Chandrabhaga
22	Beena Devi	31	5th pass	Talai	Chandrabhaga
23	Chandratari	70	Illiterate	Talai	Chandrabhaga
24	Guddi Devi	32	2nd pass	Talai	Chandrabhaga
25	Kamla Devi	63	5th pass	Talai	Chandrabhaga
26	Bimla	42	6th pass	Talai	Chandrabhaga
27	Deepa	24	B.A.	Talai	Chandrabhaga
28	Shobha	21	B.Sc.	Talai	Chandrabhaga
29	Gaytri	45	Illiterate	Talai	Chandrabhaga
30	Pushpa	21	8th pass	Talai	Chandrabhaga
31	Roshani Devi	46	Illiterate	Talai	Chandrabhaga
32	Sushila	28	5th pass	Talai	Chandrabhaga
33	Bachani Devi	55	Illiterate	Talai	Chandrabhaga
34	Devi	30	B.A.	Talai	Chandrabhaga
35	Jyoti	20	12th	Talai	Chandrabhaga
36	Nirmala	30	Illiterate	Talai	Chandrabhaga
37	Kiri Devi	60	Illiterate	Talai	Chandrabhaga
38	Champa Devi	40	5th pass	Talai	Chandrabhaga
39	Reeta	18	8th pass	Talai	Chandrabhaga
40	Gyani Devi	38	Illiterate	Talai	Chandrabhaga
41	Geeta	18	12th pass	Talai	Chandrabhaga
42	Poonam	17	10th pass	Talai	Chandrabhaga
43	Seema Devi	70	Illiterate	Bawani	Chandrabhaga
44	Kanti Devi	40	Illiterate	Bawani	Chandrabhaga
45	Munni Devi	40	Illiterate	Bawani	Chandrabhaga
46	Sukra	18	11th pass	Bawani	Chandrabhaga.
47	Srimati	65	Illiterate	Bawani	Chandrabhaga
48	Sushila	42	2nd pass	Bawani	Chandrabhaga
49	Koushalya	40	Illiterate	Bawani	Chandrabhaga
50	Madhu Devi	22	10th pass	Barani	Chandrabhaga
51	Kusum	18	10th pass	Bawani	Chandrabhaga
52	Sarada Devi	70	Illiterate	Bawani	Chandrabhaga
53	Sushila Devi	32	Illiterate	Bawani	Chandrabhaga
54	Madhu	26	6th	Bawani	Chandrabhaga

Respondent of Fakot Water Management

Sl. No.	*Name*	*Age*	*Education*	*Village*	*Watershed*
1	Sunder Devi	80	Illiterate	Bhaintan	Fakot
2	Manta Devi	20	10th pass	Bhaintan	Fakot
3	Sampati Devi	48	8th pass	Bhaintan	Fakot
4	Uma Devi	40	8th pass	Bhaintan	Fakot
5	Ashari Devi	25	8th pass	Bhaintan	Fakot
6	Bhagwan Devi	45	Illiterate	Bhaintan	Fakot
7	Pushpa Negi	35	Ist pass	Bhaintan	Fakot
8	Pyra Negi	42	5th pass	Bhaintan	Fakot
9	Vimla Negi	40	5th pass	Bhaintan	Fakot
10	Choti Negi	40	Illiterate	Bhaintan	Fakot
11	Sushila Negi	30	10th pass	Bhaintan	Fakot
12	Duma Negi	32	5th pass	Bhaintan	Fakot
13	Ujala Negi	40	5th pass	Bhaintan	Fakot
14	Mala Negi	59	5th pass	Bhaintan	Fakot
15	Manju Negi	24	10th pass	Bhaintan	Fakot
16	Meena Negi	22	10th pass	Bhaintan	Fakot
17	Jodari Negi	45	1st pass	Bhaintan	Fakot
18	Kusum	18	10th pass	Bhaintan	Fakot
19	Pintor Devi	45	1st pass	Bhaintan	Fakot
20	Chandra Devi	28	5th pass	Bhaintan	Fakot
21	Manju Negi	22	8th pass	Bhaintan	Fakot
22	Choti Negi	50	1st pass	Bhaintan	Fakot
23	Nagdai	72	Illiterate	Bhaintan	Fakot
24	Sarimagi	28	Illiterate	Bhaintan	Fakot
25	Sunita	19	8th pass	Bhaintan	Fakot
26	Rekha Negi	19	10th pass	Bhaintan	Fakot
27	Kavita Negi	18	10th pass	Bhaintan	Fakot
28	Rita Negi	18	10th pass	Bhaintan	Fakot

Abbreviations

FAO	-	Food and Agriculture Organisation
GDI	-	Gender related Development Index
IUCN	-	International Union for Conservation of Natural resources
JFM	-	Joint Forest Management
Ngo	-	Non Governement Organisation
UN	-	United Nations
UNEP	-	United Nations Environment Programme
UNDP	-	United Nations Development Programme
WHO	-	World Health Organisation

Bibliography

Acharya Sarathi, (1979), Employment of Women and Men in India: A Historical Review, 1901-1951. *The Indian Journal of Labour Economics,* VXXII, No. 3 October, pp. 138-160.

Andams, W.M. (1990) *Green Development, Environment and Sustainability in the Third World,* London Routledge.

Aggarwal, B. (1989) Rural Women, Poverty and Natural Resources: Sustenance, Sustainability and Struggle for Change, *Economic and Political Weekly,* Oct. 28, WS 46-WS65.

Ahmad, Karuna, (1979), Studies of Educational Working Women in India: Trends and Issues, *Economic and Political Weekly,* VXIV, N33, 18th August.

Ahmad, S. (1994), Report of the technical committee on drought prone area programme and desert development programme, ministry of rural development, government of India, New Delhi, pp. 73.

Anonymous (1922), Report of the Forest Grievances Committee, Government Printing Press, Allahabad, pp. 3-7.

Anonymous (1964), G.O. No. 6849/XIV-246-B-564/57 van (Kha) vibhag, dated 17-11-1964 U.P. Forest Department, Lucknow.

Anonymous (1997), Report on natural resources acconting for non marked forest produce for eight hill districts of Uttar Pradesh. Agriculture Finance Corporation, New Delhi.

Anonymous, (1995) Report of the high level committee on Westlands development. Department of wastelands development, Ministry of Rural Areas and Employment, Government of India, New Delhi, pp. 70.

Agnes, Flavia (1996) Redefining the Agenda of women's movement within a secular framework in Sarkar Tanika and Butalia Uravashi, *Women and the Hindu Right*, Kali for Women, New Delhi.

Atkinson, E.T. 1884, *The Himalayan Gazetteer*, Vol. II, III Cosmo Publication, Delhi (Reprint 1973)

Bahuguna, V.K. (1992) Collective Resource Management: An Experience in Harda Forest Divison, Regional Center for Wastelands Development, IIFM, Bhopal.

Bandhgopadhyay, J. and M. Moench (1985), "Local Needs and Forest Resources management in the Himalayas" in *India's Environment: Crises and Responses* edited by J. Bandhyopadhyay et. al, Nataraj Publishers, Dehradun, India.

Barzber, (B. 1983) *The Logic and Limits of Trust*. New Brunswick. NJ: Rutgers University press.

Bansal, R.C. and Grewal, S.S., (1986), Studies on sedimentation of Sukhna lake; corrective measures and Hydrology in annual progress, report central soil and water conservation research and training institute, research center, Chandigarh.

Bansal, R.C. (1992), Our Sukhna lake—its silt and water, status report, 1992.

Bhati, J.B. and Dr. Singh (1987), women's Contributions

to agriculture economy in Hill regions of North West India: *Economic and Poltical Weekly,* Vol. 22, No. 17 April 25, 1987

Bhumbla, D.R. Mishra, P.P. Grewal, S.S. and Mittal, S.P. (1980), Soil conservation in Sukhomajri a new direction. Proceedings of the national symposium on "Soil and Water management in 1980's" held at Dehradun, Feb, 1980, India.

Bhatt, J.L. 1995, Joint Forest Management. Employment New, 20 (37): 1-2, New Delhi.

Bhatt, B.P. Negi, A.K. and Todaria, N.P. 1994, Fuelwood consumption pattern at different altitudes in Garhwal Himalaya. *Energy,* 19(4): 465-468.

Brokenshaw, D.W. Warren, D.M. and Werner, O. (eds) (1980). *Indigenous Knowledge Systems and Development.* University Press of America, Washington, D.C.

Bryant, C. and White, L.G. (1982). *Managing Development in the Third World.* Westview, Boulder, co.

Chambers, Robert, (1983), *Rural Development Putting the Last First,* London: Longman.

Champion, H.G. and Seth, S.K. 1968, A revised survey of the Forest types in India, Government of India Publications, Delhi, p. 404.

Chauhan, D.S. 1995. People's Insitituions in panchayati forest management: lesson for joint forest management (A Case Study of Garhwal Himalaya). Project report submitted to Indian Instititute of Forest Management, Bhopal (unpublished) p. 205.

Chekki, D. (ed) (1980). *Participatory Democracy in Action: International Profiles of Community Development.* Vikas, New Delhi. India.

Chopra, K., Kadekodi, G.K. and Murty, M.N., (1990), *Participatory Development, People and Common Property Resources,* Sage, New Delhi

Chopra, Kanchan, Gopal K. Kadekodi and M.N. Murty (1988). Participatory development: An approach of the management of common property resources. Institute of Economic Growth, New Delhi, India.

Cochrane, G. (1979). *The Cultural Appraisal of Development Projects*, Praeger, New York.

Cohen, J.H. and Uphoff, N.T. (1977). Rural development participation: concepts and measures for project design, implementation and evaluation. Cornell University, Rural Development Committee, Ithaca, NY.

Corna, Michael, (1981), Modernisation and development potential of traditional grassroots peasants organizations. In Mustafa Attir, B. Helzner and Z. Suda (eds.) *Directions of Change: Modernisation Theories, Research and Realities.* Boulder Co., Westview Press, pp. 121-139.

Datta, Samar, K. (1999) Forest Resource Management, pre-workshop volume, National workshop on JFM, 25-26 Feb., organised by VIKSAT, SPWD, AKF(1) and Gujarat Forest Department, Ahmedabad, India.

Dhar, S.K. (1990), Early experiences with hill resource management societies as joint forest managers in participatory forest management in the Shiwalik hills. Experiences of the Haryana forest Department. Ford Foundation working paper N.5, New Delhi, India.

Dhar, T.N., Gupta, S.P. and Johri, S.C. 1997, Forestry in the Himalayan States of India (A comparative study). Society for Himalayan Environmental Rehabilitation and Peoples Action (SHERPA), Lucknow.

Dhyani, B.L., J.S. Sharma, G.P. Juyal, Ram Babu and K.S. Katiyar (1997), Socio-economic analysis of participatory integrated watershed management in Garhwal Himalaya, Fakot watershed. Bul No. -35/D-24, SWCRTI, Dehradun – 248195, Dehradun, India.

Eisenstadt, S.N. and Luis Roniger, (1984), *Patrons, Clients and Friends: Interpersonal Relations and the Structure of Trust in Society.* Cambridge, England: Combridge University Press.

Esmon, M. and Uphoff, N.T., (1984), *Local Organizations, Intermediaries in Rural Development.* Cornell University Press, Ithaca, New York.

F.A.O. (1995), Restoring the Balance: Women and Forest Resources, Rome, F.A.O. and Sweden SIDA.

Fernandes, W. and Menon, G. 1987 Tribal women and forest economy, deforestation, exploration and status change, Indian social institute, New Delhi.

Finsterbusch, K. (1984), 'Statistical summary of 52 AID projects: lessons on project effectiveness: College Park, M.D. University of Maryland (Mimeo).

Finsterbusch, K. And W.A. Van Wicklin III. (1982), The contribution of beneficiary participation of public Administration to development project effectiveness. *Journal of Public Administration and Development.* Vol. 7, pp. 1-23.

Fortman, L. and D. Rocheleau (1985) "women and agroforestry: Four myths and three case studies: in agro forestry system 2: 253-272, Nijhoffjunk Publishers, Netherlands, 1985.

Freeman, David M. (1990), Designing Local irrigation organisation for linking water demand with supply." In *The Social, Economic and Institutional Issues on Third World Management*, Sampath, Rajan, K. and Robert A. Young (Eds) Boulder: Westview Press, pp. 110-40.

Gadgil, M. and Guha, R. 1992, *This Fissured Land, An Ecological History of India,* Oxford University press, Delhi.

Gamer, R.E. (1976), *The Developing Nations: A Comparative Perspective.* Allyn and Bacon, Baston, M.A.

Gardner, Roy, Elinor Ostrom and James Walker (1990). "The nature of common pool resource problems", *Rationality and Society,* July 2, 3 pp. 335-58.

Gairola, T.D. 1936, Selected Revenue Decision of Kumaon. Government Press, Allahabad.

Glover, Harold, (1944), Erosion in the Punjab: its causes and cure a survey of soil conservation, *The Civil and Military Gazette,* ed. Lahore.

Gorman, Robert F., (1985), *Private Voluntary Organizations as Agents of Development,* Boulder, Co.: Westview Press.

Government of India, (1988), National Forest Policy Resolution. Informal Shramshakti, Report of the national commission on self employed women and women in the Government of India, (1988) sector, New Delhi.

Government of India, (1995), Country report, the fourth world conference on women, Beijing, 1995, Department of Women and Child Development, Ministry of Human Resource Development, New Delhi.

Government of West Bengal, (1994), Role of Forest Protection Committee in West Bengal, Department of Forest, GOWB, Calcutta.

Government of India (1985), Towards a perspective on Energy demand and supply in India. Advisory Board of Energy. Government of India, Delhi.

Govenment of Uttar Pradesh (1981). Status of Himalaya. A project report of the U.P. Govt. India, submitted to the World Bank by Watershed Management, Lucknow.

Government of Uttar Pradesh (1988), Hill Area sub-plan, Annual Plan 1988-89, Hill Development Department, Lucknow.

Gran, G. (1983), Lessons from development success : some lessons from contemporary case histories. NASPAA, Washington, DC.

Grewal, S.S. J.S. Samra, Mittal and Y. Agnihotri (1995) Sukhomajri concept of integrated watershed management. Technical Bulletin No. T-26/C-5. central soil and water conservation research centre, Chandigarh India

Gupta, J.R. (1990) Expanding Department Capacity to work with forest communities in participatory forest management in the Shiwalik hills: Experiences of the Haryana Forest Department. Ford foundation working paper No. 5, New Delhi, India.

Gupta, T. and Guleria, A. 1982, *Non-wood Forest Products in India*. Oxford and IBH Publishing Co. Pvt. Ltd. New Delhi

Haryana Forest Department, (1971), Third working plan for the forests of Pinjore Range, Ambala forest division, 1969-66 to 1977-80 by Prem Singh Malik.

Haryana Forest Department, undated, list of dams build in Morni and Ambala divison, Pinjore, Mimeo.

Hedge, N.G. and Daniel, J.N. 1993, promotion of Non wood forest produce through social Forestry. BAIF development research foundation, Pune

Heske, F. 1931, Problem der waldeshaltung in Himalaya. Tharandfer forestlichien fahrbuch, 82(8)

Hellinger, D. and Hellinger, S. (1983), Building local capacity for sustainable development. The development group for alternative policies, Washington DC.

Hobley, M. (1996) participatory forestry: the process of change in India and Nepal, rural development forestry study, guide 3, pp. 1-24 RDFN, Overseas Development Institute, London.

Honadle, G. (1981), Fishing for sustainability: the role of capacity building in development administration. Development Alternatives inc, Washington, DC.

Honadle, G. and Klauss, R. (eds) 1979. *International Development Administration: Implementation Analysis for Development Projects*, Praeger, New York.

Hondale, George, (1982), "Structural aspects of capacity building, or who gets the fish? Special supplement on integrated rural development in *Rural Development Participation Review* 3 (Spring): 1-3.

Irene Dankelman and Joan Davidson (Reprinted in 1993) women and Environment in the third world, Alliance for the future Earthscan publications Ltd., London in association with IUCN.

Jedikca, A.D. (1977), *Organisation for Rural Development: Risk taking and Appropriate Technology*. Praeger, New York.

Kaul, M.C. 1993, Durability in diversity two centuries of co-management in the Punjab forests, An institional analysis, draft paper for publication, mimeo.

Kaur, Ravinder, (1994) "women in forestry in India, policy, research and external affairs" working papers. Women in development World Bank, Washington D-C.

Kelker, G. and Nathan, D., 1991, *Gender and Tribe: Women, Land and Forests in Jharkhand*, Kali for Women, New Delhi.

Kerr, John Ganesh Pangara, Vasudha L. Pongare and P.J. George (1998) The role of watershed projects in developing rainfed agriculture in the Indian semi-arid tropics- ICAR World Bank Research Project. World Bank, New Delhi, India.

Kolawole, A. (1982) The role of Grassroots participation in National development: Lessons from the Kwara state of Nigeria: community development journal: 17(2)A learning process approach; *Public Administration Review*. 40 (5).

Korten, D.C. and Alfonso, F.B. (eds) (1981). *Bureaucracy and Poor: Closing the Gap*. McGraw-Hill, Singapore.

Kumar, A.K. (1996) "UNDP's gender-Related development Index: A computation for Indian states" *Economic and Political Weekly*, April 6, pp. 887-885.

Leach, M. (1992) 'Gender and the environment : Trap and opportunities', *Development in Practice*, vol. 2, No. 1, pp. 12-22

Laxmi Lingam (ed) (1998) *Understanding Women's Health Issues a Reader,* 1998 Kali for Women, New Delhi.

Lindsay, J.M. (1994) Law and community in the management of India's state forest. Working papers, Cambridge, Lioncoln Institutute of Land Policy.

Lchmann, N. (1980), *Trust and Power,* New York: John Wiley.

Malguire, R. (1981), *Bottom-up Development in Haiti.* Inter-American Foundations, Rosslyn, VA.

Malhotra, K.C. Deb, D., Dutta, M. Vasuler, T-S., Yadav, G. and Adhikari, M., (1992) Role of non-Timber Forest Produce in Village Economy, IBRAD, Calcutta.

Malhotra, K.C., M. Poffenberger, A. Bhattacharya, and D. Dev (1992) Rapid Rural Appraisal Methodology Trails in Southwest Bengal: assessing Natural Forest Regeneration patterns and nonwood forest product harvesting practices, sustainable management working paper No. 11, New Delhi.

Meehan, E-J (1979), *In Partnership with people: An Alternative Development Strategy.* Inter American Foundation, Rosslyn, VA.

Mencher, Joan and K. Sardamoni (1982), "Muddy Feet and Dirty Hands. Rice production and Female Agricultural labour", *Economic and Political Weekly,* December 25.

Mies, M. et al. (1983), "Landless women organisea case study of an organisation in rural Andhra", *Manushi,* vol. 3, No. 3 March-April.

Millikan; Max, Lucian Pye and Douglas Hapgood. (1966), *The Role of Participation in Development,* MIT, Center for International Studies Cambridge.

Minoti, Chakravarty, Kaul (1996). *Common Lands and Customary Laws: Institional Changes in North India over the Past Two Centuries,* Oxford University Press, New Delhi, India.

Mishra, P.R. and Sarin, M. 1987, Social security through social fencing: Sukhomajri and Nada's Road to self sustaining development, paper presented at I.I.E.D. conference of sustainable development, April 28-30, 1987, London.

Mittal, S.P., Sud A.D., Samra, J.S., Grewal, S.S. and Singh, G. 1991, Grasses for soil conservation in Shiwalik hills, CSWCRTI Research centre, Chandigarh.

Mittal, S.P. Grewal, S.S., Agnihotri, Y. and Mishra, P.R. (1980), Study for mass mobilisation and people's participation in the implementation of watershed management programme. Presented at seminar on "Strategy for mass mobilization ans people's participation" organised by CBIP, New Delhi, Oct. 28-30, 1980, India.

Moser, C.O.N. (1991), "Gender planning in the third world: Meeting Practical and Strategic Needs" in R. Grant and K. Newland, eds. *Gender and International Relations,* Milton Keynes; Open University Press, pp. 83-21.

Myers M., R. David, S. Akrot and A. Hamld (1995) "The effect of male out migration on women's management of natural resources in the Sudan" paper no. 60, IIED, London.

Myers, N. 1996, The World's Forests: problems and potentials. *Environmental Conservation,* 23 (2): 156-168.

Negi, A.K., Bhatt, B.P. Todaria, N.P. and Saklani, A. 1997. The effect of colonialism on forests and the local people in Garhwal Himalaya, India. *Mountain Research and Development,* 17(2): 159-168.

Niraj Kumar, (2000), All is not green with JFM in Indian Forest, *Trees and People Newsletter* No. 42, pp. 46-50.

Okly, Peter and David Marsden, (1984), Approaches to participation in rural development. Geneva: Interntional Labour Office.

Olson, M. (1965). *The Logic of Collective Action.* Harvard University Press, Massachusetts, Cambridge.

Olson, M. (1982) *The Rise and Decline of Nations: Economic Growth, Stagnation and Social Rigidities.* Yale University Press, New Heaven and London.

Panda A., Dabas, M. Varalakshmi, V., Shah, V.N. and Gupta, J.R., 1992, Grass yield under community participation in Haryana Shiwaliks, JFM Series No. 1, HFD/TERI, New Delhi.

Pant, G.B. 1922. *The Forest Problems in Kumaon,* Government Press, Allahabad, pp. 40-65.

Patil, B.R. (1982), "People's participation in development". A working paper of the Council for Social Development, New Delhi.

Pauw, E.K. 1896, Report on the tenth settlement of Garhwal district, Government Press, Allahabad.

Pearson, G.T. 1869, Report on the forests of Garhwal and Kumaon Government press, Allahabad, p. 13.

Poffenberger, M. (1990), "Joint management for forest lands: experiences from south Asia." A Ford Foundation programme statement

Poffenberger, M. and Chhatrapati Singh (1996) Communities and State: Re-establishing the balance in Indian Forest policy, in *Village Voices, People Choices,* (ed. M. Poffenberger and Betsy McGean) Oxford University Press, New Delhi.

Poffenberger, M. and Sarin, (1990), Fiber grass from Forest land: A case from North India, Ford Foundation, working paper No. 10, New Delhi.

Prasad, J. (1999) Institutions in JFM programme, pre-workshop volume, National workshop on JFM, 25-26 Feb, organised by VIKSAT, SPWD, AKF(1), and Gujarat Forests department, Ahmadabad.

Rajput, P. and L. Swarup, (1995) *Women and Globalization,* Ashish publishing house, New Delhi, India.

Raju, G. (1999) People's Institutions in Joint forest management, pre-workshop volume, National workshop on JFM, 25-26 Feb, organised by VIKSAT, SPWD, AKF(1) and Gujarat Forest department, Ahmadabad.

Raju, G., R. Vaghela, and M.S. Raju (1993) development of people's institions for management of forests, VIKSAT, Ahmadabad.

Raturi, H.K. 1910, Garhwal varnan, Bombay, India.

Ravindranath, N.H., M. Gadgil and J. Campbell (1992) economic and econlogical aspects of afforestation programmes. Paper presentation at the SPWD workshop on joint forest management at Surajkund, SPWD, New Delhi.

Rawat, A.S. 1991 History of Forest management: conflicts and their impact in the central Himalaya. In Rawat, A.S. (ed.), *History of Forestry in India,* pp. 280-325.

Redcliff, M. (1987), Sustainable development exploring the contradiction. London: Methuen.

Richardson, Ann. (1983), Participation (concepts is social policy 1) London: Routledge and Kegan.

Report of the team for the study of Community Projects and National Extension Service, volume 1, Committee on Plan Projects, New Delhi, November, 1997, pp. 137-138.

Report of the Committee on Panchayati Raj Institutions (Chairman: Ashoka Mehta), Department of Rural Development, Ministry of Agriculture and Irrigation, Government of India, (1978), pp.141-142.

Report of the working group on development of village level organisation of rural women, department of rural development, ministry of agriculture and irrigation, Government of India, June, 1978, pp. 4-21.

Report of the working group on development of village organizations of rural women, government of India,

Ministry of Agriculture and irrigation, Department of Rural Development, June, 1978, pp. 3-4.

Ritter, Archibold, R.M. and David, H. Pollock, (1983), Latin American prospects for the 1980's : Equity, Democratization and development, New York: Praeger.

Rogers, B. (1989) *The Demonstration of Women: Discrimination in Developing Societies,* Tavistock Publications, 1989.

Roy Burman, J.J. (1999) A Critical Note on the Joint Forest Management policies, Pre-workshop volume, National Workshop on JFM, 25-26 Feb, organised by VIKAT, SPWD, AKF(1) and Gujarat department, Ahmedabad.

Rubinstein, R. (1994) Collective violence and common security. In T., Ingold (ed) *Companion Encyclopedia of Anthropology,* Routledge, London, pp. 983-1009.

Saklani, A. 1987, the History of a Himalayan princely state: Change, conflicts and awakening, Durga publishers, Delhi.

Samra, J.S. (2001) Participatory watershed management, yojana, Vol. 45, No. 1, pp. 24-27.

Samra, R.C. Bansal, A.K. Sikka, S.P. Mittal and Y. Agnihotri (1995), resources conservation through watershed management in shiwalik Foothills, Bul. No. T-28/C-7, CSWCRTI, RC, Chandigarh – 160019 (India).

Sarin, M. (1996). Joint Forest Management: The Haryana Experience Centre for environment education Ahmedabad, India.

Sarin, M. (1993) From conflict to collaboration: Local institutions in Joint Forest Management. JFM working paper No. 14, National support group of Joint forst management, SPWD, New Delhi.

Sarin, M. (1996) Actions of the voiceless: The challenge of addressing subterranean conflicts related to marginalised groups and women in community forestry paper presented at the electronics conference on addressing natural resources conflicts through community forestry, January-May, 1996, FAO/FT PP, ROME.

Sarin, M. (1995), Delving beneath the surface; latent gender based conflicts in community forestry Institutions, Paper written for the FTPP, FAF, ROME.

Saxena, K.G., Rao, K.S. and Purohit, A.N. 1993, sustainable forestry: prospects in India. *Journal of Sustainable Forestry*, 1(2): 69-95.

Saxena, N.C. 1987 Common, Trees and the poor in the Uttar Pradesh Hills, oversease development institute, London.

Saxena, N.C. (1997) The saga of participatory forest management in India. CIFOR, Jakarta.

Saxena, N.C. (1999) The new Forest policy and joint forest management in India, Pre-workshop volume, National workshop on JFM, 25-26 Feb. organised by VIKSAT, SPWD, AKF(1) and Gujarat Forest Department, Ahmedabad.

Shah, S.L. 1996, Issues relating to sustainable land use in Uttarakhand, Learing lesson of multi-disciplinary action research in land use management. In Kumar, K. Dhyani, P.P. and palni, L.M.S. (eds.) Land utilization in the central Himalaya. HIMVIKAS Publication No -8, pp. 53-74.

Singh, K. and Ballabh, V. 1991, people's participation in forest management: experience of Van Panchayats in U.P. Hills wasteland News, August – October pp. 5-14.

Singhal, R.M. 1993, Social forestry and participatory forest management in India. Van vigyan 31(182): 26-34.

Somanathan, E. 1991, Deforestation, property rights and incentives in central Himalaya westlands news, August-October, pp. 14-27.

Stowell, V.A. 1907 A manual of the land Tenures of Kumaon division Allahabad, U.P. India.

Swarn Lata Arya and J.S. Samra (2001). Revisiting watershed Management Institutios in Haryana Shiwaliks, India, (SWCRTI, Chandigarh-160019 (India).

Swarn Lata Arya and J. S. Samra (1995)- "Socio-economic implications and participatory appraisal of integrated watershed management project at Bunga" Technical Bulletin No. T-27/C-6, Central soil and water conservation research and training institution research and training institute, research centre, chandigarh, India.

Swarn Lata Arya, (1995), "Soil and water conservation programme farm women burdened by development initiatives". *Indian Farming*, Vol. 44, No. 10, pp. 27-30.

Swarup, R. 1993, agricultural economy of Himalayn region Vol. II, Garhwal. HIMVIKAS publication No. 5, p. 223. Gyanodaya Prakashan, Nainital-U.P.

Taylor, Ellen and Cynthia moore, (1980), "Para-professionals in rural development" reality and potential. *Rural Deveopment Participation Review* 2 (Fall): 1-6.

Thakur, D.S. (1988), "Himachali women" givers of food, forgiver of society", *Indian Farming,* Vol. XXXVII, No. 8, pp. 306.

The state of forest report, 1991, 1993, 1995. Forest Survey of India, Dehradun.

The Punjab Minor Canals Act. 1905 (Punjab Act. III of 1905), 7th April 1905: 1st June, 1905, Punjab Govt. Gazette, pp. 246-284.

Tucker, Richard P., (1984), "The Historical context of social forestry in the Kumaon Himlayas". The Journal of developing. Areas, 18 April: 341-356.

Uberoy, A. (1994), "Science and Technology projects for women in agriculture–An Evaluation report". Sponsored by National Commission for Women, December 1994.

UNDP (1980) "Rural women's participation in Development" Evaluation study No. 3, United Nations Development Programme, New York, June 1980.

Uphoff, Norman, (1992), Local Institional Development An Analytical source Book with cases. West Hartford, Conn.: Kumarian press.

Venkateswaran, S. (1995), *Environment, Development and the Gender Gap*, Sage Publications, New Delhi, India.

Walton, H.G. (1911a) *Almora: A Gazetteer,* Government Press, Allahabad.

Walton, H.G. (1911b), *British Garhwal: A Gazetteer.* Government Press, Allahabad.

Wantrup Ciriacy, S.V. and Bishop, R.C. (1975), "Common property as a concept in Natural resource policy". *Natural Resource Journal,* 15, pp. 713-27.

World Bank (1995) "The World Bank Gand Gender in India." A World Bank Country Study, Washington D.C. World Bank.

Zaman, W.C. (1984), Public participation in Development and health programmes: Lessons from rural Bangladesh, University Press of America, Lanhan, M.A.

ZSI 1995, *Fauna of Rajaji National Park,* Zoological Survey of India, Calcutta.

Index